Ordering Information:

Quantity sales. Special discounts are available on quantity purchases by corporations, associations, and others. For details, contact the publisher at the address above. For orders by U.S. trade bookstores and wholesalers. Please contact Amazon at www.amazon.com.

Printed in the United States of America

To my wife, my partner, my friend.

Many thanks are due to Robin Z., who schlepped a copy of this book from London to Israel to Hong Kong (and places in between) while proofreading it in incredible detail. Your Oxford education dwarfs mine, especially in the finer nuances of language. As Shaw said, "The English and the Americans are two peoples divided by a common Language." I cannot thank you enough.

Also many sincere thanks to Susan H., who proofread and found even more mistakes than anyone else found! Your selfless efforts are truly appreciated.

Additional thanks to Rick B. who has been instrumental in making this book look good and generating the Kindle version.

Table of Contents

Foreword i

Preface vi

Chapter 1 – Why the 12 Steps haven't worked for you. 1
The 12 Step process hasn't worked for you. Why? 2
Why is recovery from food addiction so hard? 3
Who is this book for? 7
How this book is structured 10

Chapter 2 – My Story 13

Chapter 3 – Step 1: Waving the white flag 29
Believing It IS a disease and that it is HARD 29
What is the disease and how does it manifest itself? 33
What kind of pain do you want? 40
How exactly am I powerless over it? 44

Chapter 4 – Step 2: Back to our Senses 47
My Own Best Efforts 47
Sponsorship: A bridge between the 2nd and 3rd Steps. 49
Picking a sponsor 50

Chapter 5 – Step 3: Where Reality and Theory Meet 55
Finding a Higher Power – of your understanding 58
The gifts of finding a Higher Power 62

Chapter 6 – The Decision Made, We Need Tools 67
Food Plan and Goal Weight 68
Plan of Eating 72
Action Plan 79
Writing 82
Meetings 84
A warning about meetings 86
Phone Meetings, Online Meetings and Podcasts 90
The Telephone as a Tool 92

Literature.. 93
Summing up so far.. 94

Chapter 7 – Steps 4 & 5: Moving out of neutral................... 95
Fear of the 4th Step.. 96
Doing a 4th Step 97
Resentments.. 99
Fears..101
Sex...101
Some final thoughts on a 4th Step.......................................101
Step 5 – Giving it all Away 102

Chapter 8 – Steps 6 & 7: We're not Perfect after all 105
Character Defects: the Disease's Arsenal.............................107
Immaturity 107
Narcissism, Ego and Self-centeredness................................110
Control Issues 113
Intellectualism and Cynicism..114
Perfectionism...115
Fear of Success/Fear of Unknown Repercussions 116
6th Step – Summing Up...116
Step 7 – Asking for Help 117

Chapter 9 – Steps 8 & 9: Facing your Past............................121
Step 9: Facing Your Past...122

Chapter 10 – Steps 10 & 11: Toward the program ideal...........127
Step 11 – Adjusting our will to reality 130

Chapter 11 – Step 12: Trust God and Work with Another 137
Service..137
Sponsorship 140
Carrying the message to those not yet in program...............142
Practicing These Principles 145

Chapter 12 – The Elephant in the Room: Sexuality.................149
Attractiveness..150
Self esteem 151

Fear of Success – and Attention:..155

Sexuality..158

Intimacy and Love 161

Sex in Marriage...165

Relationships 168

Friendship relationships...170

Chapter 13 – Stopping your next Slip or are you in it?.............173

What to do when the urge to eat hits.....................................176

Dealing with Relapse – the 12th Step Within...........................178

Chapter 14 – Two Last Important Topics..................................181

Getting Outside Help...181

Switching addictions 183

Chapter 15 – The Final Gift (What's in it for me?) 187

APPENDIX I – Helpful slogans and phrases 195

APPENDIX II – Other helpful items..196

Foreword

Eating disorders, compulsive overeating, anorexia and bulimia, are very prevalent in western society. The rates of obesity in the United States have been climbing in recent decades. More than a third of adults are obese. Obesity rates in minority populations are even higher.[1]

Eating disorders demand a heavy toll on those who suffer. The mortality rate for anorexia (4%) is 12 times higher than for all other causes of death for women aged 15 to 24 combined.[2] Obesity is a primary factor in numerous chronic health conditions such as diabetes, heart disease, and cancer. It is one of the leading preventable causes of death. Every year Americans spend over 40 billion dollars on diets and weight loss products. Yet, the vast majority of people who attempt to diet end up relapsing and gaining back their weight or developing anorexia or bulimia. [3]

Those in O.A. and other food programs are well aware of the anguish and despair rendered by eating disorders. They come into the program with feelings of intense shame and remorse for their eating and weight. Many have lost jobs or have conflicts with families and loved ones. They often feel isolated and unable to connect with others. Some have attempted suicide. Others feel profoundly empty and as if their life had no purpose. It is this pain that brings people in to 12 Step programs. Coming into the rooms, people feel immediate relief because of the power of hearing others who share their affliction and speak the same language. They stay in the hopes of finding some respite and recovery from their disordered eating and other life problems that are associated with the eating problems.

The A.A. Big Book[4] distinguished between problem drinkers and "real alcoholics." Recent research has validated this hypothesis and found that many problem drinkers are helped by a variety of behavioral and psychological interventions. A small minority of drinkers do not respond well to most interventions. It seems that these people, the real alcoholics, seem to have the best chance at recovery using 12 Step programs.

Rozanne S., the founder of O.A., was aware of the phenomenon of Alcoholics Anonymous when she contacted some other women in the hopes of supporting each other in their weight loss. Recognizing similarities between the compulsion to drink in alcoholism and their own obsession with food and dieting, the earliest members sought out members of A.A. to gain from their experience, strength and hope. Observing the prevalence of people with weight problems, Rozanne envisioned that O.A. would be bigger than A.A. [5] She saw how the Twelve Steps could provide recovery in the physical, emotional, and spiritual realm. The early successes of the first members lead to the growth of O.A. into an international organization with chapters in 75 countries.

It is important to understand the difference between poor eating habits and a true compulsion to over (or under) eat. The rates of obesity and eating disorders in general are at all-time highs. There are some obese or underweight people who respond to diets or behavior modification. Overeaters Anonymous is a program designed to help the "real compulsive overeaters," the ones who don't seem to benefit from these direct interventions. Many members of O.A. talk of how they have tried and failed at diet after diet. Members often refer to the program as "the last house on the block."

Recovery from chronic conditions such as alcoholism or compulsive overeating is difficult and relentless. As it says in the Big Book, many have sought an "easier softer way." Many transplants from A.A. to O.A. assume that addressing their eating issues will be a "piece of cake" compared to their drinking or drug problems. However, many cross-addicted people report that compulsive overeating seems to be more persistent than alcohol or drug dependency. There is a creeping, insidious nature of a food addiction that is often hard to see clearly. Alcoholics know when they have had a slip, but a compulsive overeater often can't tell the difference between a bad food day and a relapse.

For compulsive overeaters, the lure of commercial diet programs, specialty foods and medical intervention is often apocryphal and can lead to even further demoralization. Many hold out the hope that their weight problems are simply related to poor habits or temporary situations that are easily resolved. Additionally, there are some fundamental differences between eating difficulties and alcoholism. Although it can be challenging, an alcoholic can entirely avoid drinking alcohol for the rest of his life. A compulsive overeater must continue to eat in order to remain alive. Most people do not develop alcoholism until their late teens, early twenties or even later, but many people with eating issues report disordered eating in early childhood.

A particularly interesting aspect of compulsive overeating is that because over or under eating results in changes in the body, compulsive overeating is not as anonymous as other addictions might be. This is a paradox because compulsive overeaters tend to isolate and usually wish to avoid any attention to themselves. Beginning a recovery program adds specific challenges as food is intertwined in almost all aspects of our lives and attempts to make food less of a focus can result in someone feeling more isolated. Additionally, particularly if someone is significantly overweight, starting to eat more healthfully may only serve to focus attention on personal discomfort with one's body (that previously had been masked by the overeating). People may remain at unhealthy weights for a long time, and continue to suffer the effects of their neglect of themselves, even if they are eating well and following all the suggestions of the program.

For these reasons and more, recovery from compulsive overeating is particularly challenging. It requires more sustained effort and vigilance, particularly in the early stages of recovery. Relapse rates for all addictions are quite significant and it seems that eating disorders have even higher relapse and higher dropout rates than other addictions. However, it is also true that there are many people who have managed to address their compulsive overeating and maintained healthy weights for many years. This book explores how these people have been successful in using the 12 Steps to arrest their addictive relationship with food.

It is important to understand the food relapse cycle and how many people find themselves at a loss regarding the 12 Steps. This book reviews how the 12 Steps work and why they sometimes don't. It examines common fallacies and missteps that people take and how that can impact their recovery. Through stories and personal reflections, this book identifies what actions people with long-term recovery have done over the course of their recovery. The book also comments on some of the reasons that some people have no success finding long-term recovery, despite great effort.

Overeaters Anonymous and programs like it have been an essential part of recovery from compulsive overeating for thousands of people of many ethnic and cultural backgrounds all around the world. Working the program can be difficult and recovery can be tenuous, however, there are many examples of people who have used the 12 Steps to gain freedom from compulsive eating as well as spiritual and psychological growth. I wish the reader strength and hope in their recovery.

– Harriet Boxer, Ph.D.

References

1. Mitchinson, D., Hay, P., Slewa-Younan, S., Mond, J. *The Changing Demographic Profile of Eating Disorder Behaviors in the Community* BMC Public Health. 2014;14(943) http://www.biomedcentral.com/1471-2458/14/943 (December 10, 2014)

2. National Association of Anorexia and Related Disorders http://www.anad.org/get-information/about-eating-disorders/eating-disorders-statistics/ (December 10, 2014)

3. Centers for Disease Control and Prevention. http://www.cdc.gov/obesity/data/adult.html (December 10, 2014).

4. Alcoholics Anonymous: The Story of How Many Thousands of Men and Women Have Recovered from Alcoholism (4th Edition). (2001) Alcoholics Anonymous World Services, Inc. New York.

5. Beyond our Wildest Dreams: A History of Overeaters Anonymous as Seen by a Cofounder. (1996) Overeaters Anonymous Inc. Rio Rancho, NM.

Preface

This book is written for those who have had some experience with the 12 Steps, especially as it pertains to compulsive eating and relapse. It is my hope that anyone may benefit from reading this book, however some of the terminology contained within might seem a bit baffling to those unfamiliar with the 12 Steps. We 12 Steppers have something of "a language of our own." Using this language is not meant to exclude anyone, but is more of a "shorthand" we use to express concepts we mutually understand. Since I am assuming that the reader has attended meetings in one of these programs, consequently I go into some concepts that are best understood by attending meetings for compulsive eaters.

There are a number of 12 Step programs for compulsive eaters. Their membership numbers vary, as does the number of meetings around the country. The largest of these is Overeaters Anonymous (O.A.), which has the most meetings in the most places. Other programs include Compulsive Eaters Anonymous-HOW (CEA-HOW), Food Addicts Anonymous (FAA), Gray Sheet Anonymous (GSA), Eating Disorders Anonymous, and I'm sure I've missed a few.

There are other *non*-12 Step programs (most of which are commercial), but since this book concerns 12 Step recovery for compulsive eating (overeating, bulimia, and anorexia), we won't be talking about them. Suffice it to say that most emphasize only the weight loss and behavior modification associated with the eating alone. 12 Step programs, while addressing the physical aspect of the disease, also address the emotional and spiritual deficit most of us had within us during our active eating days. 12 Step programs also work on changing people in ways beyond their eating behaviors. They work on helping their members become better people, which in turn leads to a much healthier person – healthy in body, mind and spirit.

A quick comparison of the various food centered 12 Step programs before continuing might be helpful. O.A. does not have a specific food plan, although it does have several food plans outlined in a pamphlet entitled "*The Dignity of Choice.*" These food plans are all pretty common sense food plans, and members are free to use them or not use them. However, O.A. does stress that members should find *some* food plan to follow. Many members additionally consult with a doctor or nutritionist, an outside food planning program such as "Weight Watchers," or with their sponsor. I believe there is at least one other 12 Step program that does not stress a specific food plan.

Some of the other 12 Step programs I mentioned are more structured and involved food plans that their members must follow to be considered abstinent. Some also insist that members have a sponsor and often have other requirements to be members in good standing. Additionally, some of these programs are more stringent than others. I should mention that since these programs all follow the 12 Steps and 12 Traditions, the only requirement for membership in all programs is "*a desire to stop eating compulsively.*" However, some prohibit non-abstinent members from sharing at meetings and sponsoring.

I have observed some of these programs, and I believe each has its strengths and its weaknesses. Since I have not attended meetings in all programs, I will speak a bit in generalities, although I can speak with authority concerning the programs I have attended – one with a specific food plan and one with no specific food plan.

Since 12 Step members practice the Tradition of anonymity, I will not disclose in this book which programs I currently attend or which programs I have attended in the past. Throughout my years in recovery, I have gone to numerous 12 Step meetings, and mention doing so throughout the book. Just because I say I have attended a meeting of a particular 12 Step program does not mean I am or was a member. Please do not draw any conclusions as to my membership in any specific 12 Step program.

The programs with specific food plans tend to exhibit a stronger sense of recovery at their meetings. Since only abstinent members can share, the meetings seem to have strong recovery. The members at these meetings take their abstinence very seriously – as seriously as alcoholics in A.A. take their sobriety – and this was a definite plus for me. Another plus was seeing a lot of people with good physical recovery. Again, those people tended to be the ones sharing and speaking at meetings.

However, having attended one of these stricter programs for a number of years, I can tell you that there can be a downside to a program with a sometimes razor's edge definition of abstinence. Many people could not maintain such a strict abstinence over a long period of time. While the program promised physical recovery in return for a strict adherence to the food plan, once that goal was met, people often then saw the food plan as an authority figure and rebelled against it. And when a person did break his or her abstinence and had to start over, he or she often went out with an agenda of "making up for lost time." This led to a steady stream of people coming to program, leaving program, and returning to program – over and over. People in the middle of a slip rarely continued to attend meetings.

At the meetings I attended of this stricter program, there was far more emphasis on the physical recovery than on the spiritual and emotional aspects spoken about in the various Step books and the Big Book of Alcoholics Anonymous (which I will call "the Big Book" for the rest of this book). I have been told that this is not the case with this program in all areas of the country, but it was certainly the case where I attended meetings. At the meetings I attended, people got up, stated the length of their abstinence, as well as their weight loss. Their "pitches" (what they said at meetings) were most often about the weight loss benefits of sticking to the food plan.

The problem with a program where people are coming and going and not working on the inner work on which the Steps focus is that it doesn't bring a lot of emotional and spiritual growth – hence the relapses. As is said, *nothing changes if nothing changes.*

There are also programs without specific food plans, the largest being O.A. From what I have observed, sometimes these meetings seem not as strong, with a smaller percentage of members exhibiting full physical recovery than those in the other programs. One reason is that in programs like O.A., there is no abstinence requirement to be able to pitch at meetings. People who are still eating – and who don't exhibit a lot of recovery (physically or emotionally) – can sometime "bring down" a meeting. Some people in these types of programs also sometimes exhibit a very cavalier attitude about their abstinence and breaking it. Unlike the other, stricter programs, people in the middle of slips stay in the rooms, and often pitch about their slips while still in them. Coming from another program where people in the middle of slips were advised to listen (I believe the exact phrase often used was "*take the cotton out of your ears and put it in your mouth*"), I'm not sure this unequivocal inclusiveness adds much to the meetings and makes newcomers question the program's effectiveness.

On the other hand, the people who *are* finding recovery in programs that don't stress a uniform food plan tend to exhibit *very* good recovery on all levels. This is due to a stronger emphasis on the Steps and doing the "*inner work.*" The people doing the work in these programs often seem to have "gotten" the Steps better than many A.A. members. It has been my observation that while many A.A. members do the work as the Steps suggest, there are also a lot of A.A. members who are just happy that they're not drinking. Those members don't feel compelled to use the A.A. program for spiritual and emotional recovery.

If you have had experience and a predilection for one of these programs, I'm sure you agree with my description of their positive aspects and disagree with my criticisms of your particular program. However, I have tried to be as objective as humanly possible with my (obviously) subjective analysis of them.

The main thing I wanted to do with this book was to share my observations of over 30 years in 12 Step programs. This amount of time in program has allowed me to observe what works and what does not work when it comes to recovery from compulsive eating. As with everything else, these are my opinions and you can feel free to disagree. The pages ahead of you will lay out these thoughts in detail.

Chapter 1 – Why the 12 Steps haven't worked for you.

My name is John and I am a compulsive overeater.

Actually, I've been an overeater, an undereater, a bulimic, an exercise bulimic, and for an incredibly brief time, an anorexic. I manipulated my diet and my exercise for years in a vain attempt to beat the disease of compulsive eating. Luckily, 30-plus years ago, I found the 12 Steps. My first program involved alcohol, but soon afterwards I realized I had to address something that had been a lifelong problem: food. Since that time, I have been a member of one of a number of different food programs. I will talk somewhat about the comparisons of some of these programs, but I will mainly talk about Overeaters Anonymous (O.A.), because it is – by far – the largest.

When I talked to people about doing a book about finding recovery from compulsive eating, they all thought it was a good idea. There are a lot of compulsive eaters who don't know about the 12 Step solution that need help. *"What about all those people who have already come to 12 Step programs and not been successful?"* I asked. *"Don't they need help too?"*

Does the 12 Step process work for food?

When people ask me, "Do the 12 Steps work for compulsive eating?" I answer with an adamant "Absolutely!"

I live in Los Angeles, which was the birthplace for the first 12 Step program for food, Overeaters Anonymous. There are thriving meetings of as many as four different 12 Step programs for food addicts. At two of my home meetings, I see upwards of a hundred or so people a week in varying stages of recovery. Many have 20, 30 and even 40 years of abstinence.

When I say recovery, what exactly do I mean? Firstly, they are free from the bondage of food, so that it doesn't consume their entire lives. They eat, they enjoy their food, but it is in the right place within their lives. Moreover, they are maintaining a healthy body weight thanks to that freedom from obsession. Most importantly, they are _happy_. They maintain vibrant, full lives with fulfilling jobs, social lives, and families that love them.

In the end, isn't that what we all want?

Recovery is not about getting thin, it's about getting _better_ – physically, emotionally and spiritually. We look to heal the wounds – some of them embedded very deeply – that had become dysfunctional building blocks for our personalities. It also often means changing the course of our lives. Somewhere in our past – whether thanks to our parents, or other adults, or possibly ourselves – we got pointed in the wrong direction. It's not until we realize we're not going where we want to be going that we can set about changing the trajectory.

When I started in my first 12 Step program, I heard about "spiritual recovery," and the phrase almost made me bolt for the door. I know now that the word "spiritual" is not always just about God, but also about us – our _spirit_. It's about being happy, content, at peace with ourselves, at peace with others, and free of fear as much as humanly possible. In the end, it's also about becoming better human beings – towards others, but mainly toward ourselves.

I often hear newcomers say that they _hope_ the 12 Steps are their answer. I tell them that hope is for newcomers, I have faith. I have seen it work and believe it can work for anybody – if they are willing to take direction.

But so far...

The 12 Step process hasn't worked for you. Why?

The next question that usually arises after I answer "Absolutely!" to the question about the 12 Steps working for food is: "_For everyone?_" To which I answer – just as adamantly – "Absolutely _NOT!_"

Sadly, in the 30-plus years I have attended 12 Step programs for food, I have watched tens of thousands of people come and go – most with limited or no success. Some of these people came in and had what I consider the typical 12 Step food story: they entered program, had instant success, and then slipped. They spend the next few years trying desperately to get back what they once had – to no avail.

Others will get recovery for a few years, then they will lose it, then get it back again for a few years, then lose it again. Some just come to meetings, waiting for the Abstinence Fairy to whack them on the head with the Abstinence Wand. Sadly, many of the food programs inadvertently promote this behavior with the "Keep Coming Back" mantra. "Keep Coming Back," they all chime in – over and over. I can tell you that in other programs mostly for drugs and alcohol, there is a different mantra: "There's the door. When you're ready to get better, we have a solution."

Those other programs are not mean spirited or hard hearted. They just know that until a person is ready to surrender, sometimes the worst thing you can do is keep people _just_ comfortable enough to not be willing to go to any lengths to get better. I have personally seen this through the years: people who convince themselves that they are working at recovery by simply coming to meetings. As a member in another program said once "Any damned fool can navigate the doorway!"

My favorite line is "I'm praying for the willingness to stop." As a woman said at a workshop I attended once: "When it comes to addiction, willingness is _highly_ overrated!" And it's true. If Bill W. and Dr. Bob had waited until they were _willing_ to stop drinking, there still wouldn't be an Alcoholics Anonymous!

Is it true that you hear the occasional story of a person who sat around then got struck abstinent? Yes, but those stories are rare. Unfortunately, for every one of those stories, there are 20 or 30 people sitting in meetings waiting for that exact lightning to hit them. And what happens? _It doesn't._ Eventually, they get discouraged and leave, becoming convinced that the 12 Steps won't work for them and possibly don't work for eaters in general.

Why is recovery from food addiction so hard?

One of the things that is important to realize about recovery from food addiction – and this is especially true if you've come from another 12 Step program – is this important fact: _this is hard!_ Recovery from food addiction – not all the time, but in the beginning particularly – can be very, very difficult.

Addictive diseases have many weapons in their arsenals, but food has more of them. Firstly, no matter how bad an alcoholic, addict or whatever was, they probably didn't pick up that substance or habit until their teens at the earliest. Food, however, goes all the way back to the beginning. It represents mother, nurture, peace, contentment, love, approval, and reward (to name a few). Almost everyone has happy memories of meals and food at some point. Most of us remember hearing "If you are good, you'll get <fill in the goodie>."

Here's another simple fact: we all _have_ to eat! In a way, I find the phrase "food addict" humorous. Think about it – have you ever met anyone that has "kicked" the food habit? I know people say "alcoholics have to drink, they just don't drink alcohol." Speaking for this alcoholic, I've never had a drink of any liquid that then made me think about drinking alcohol. On the other hand, when I've been upset and not in a fit spiritual condition, I've had abstinent meals that made me want to keep eating.

If you're in a food program like O.A. which doesn't have a specific food plan dictated, you have another problem: the ambiguous nature of some abstinences. It's not like A.A. people don't have slips. I can tell you that if a person has a slip in A.A., he _knows_ he's having one. I've known people in O.A. who have had problems with their food for months before realizing it!

Another factor weighing against your recovery is the proliferation of "easier, softer ways." Most of society has come to believe the 12 Step method is the most effective for recovery from alcoholism and drug addiction. That means that groups like A.A. and N.A. have little competition. There aren't a lot of alternative groups out there trying to convince alcoholics that they can drink safely again. If there were, my guess is every alcoholic would have at least given it a shot before making it to A.A. Now imagine that there are hundreds, even thousands of such alternatives. That's part of the problem a compulsive eater faces. The plethora of "easier, softer ways" that constantly bombard the active compulsive eater is staggering. There is a billion dollar industry out there trying to convince eater that they can – _wait for it_ – have their cake and eat it too.

My disease also likes to use the wonderful weapon of minimization. "After all, it's _just food_!" it will try to tell me. Eating and even overeating is socially acceptable. Ever watch some of that food porn that passes as TV commercials? They're almost _begging_ you to overeat. You don't see this with booze. "Please drink responsibly" is what you hear. Where is that with food?

People who have no need for 12 Step programs seem to grasp the concept of addiction when it comes to drugs and alcohol. With food... not so much. If I go to a party and the hostess offers me a drink and I mention that I'm in recovery – the response is a ridiculous level of over-compensation. "I'm so sorry!" she'll say. "I *really* didn't know. I hope I didn't cause a problem!" *(Yes ma'am, 30 years of sobriety and your mention of a drink was all that it took for me to chuck it all away.)*

Cut to that same party an hour later and that same hostess offers me a piece of cake. "No thanks," I reply. "I'm also in a food program and don't eat sugar." What do I get as a response? "Oh, come on... you can have a *little* bit!" *Sigh.*

Even in A.A., people who should understand do not. I mentioned to an alcoholic friend that I had to speak at a meeting for compulsive eating and he said, "You? But you're not fat." I looked back and said "Yes, and you attend A.A. meetings and you're not drunk!"

For those of us with other addictions, we have even one more excuse as we go to eat: "Well, at least I'm not... drinking or drugging (or fill in the blank)." I can use *that* excuse up to 400 pounds or more on the way to dying a slower death. The fact was – for me – that since I was a compulsive eater *and* an alcoholic, as long as I continued to eat, I was not sober. The A.A. Big Book says that sobriety is and was *soundness of mind*. How sound was my thinking as I continued to eat compulsively, knowing all the time that it was a self-destructive act?

A number of years back, I read about a study done on rats concerning addiction. The study tested a number of addictive substances to see which affect the rats the most. What do you think? Heroin? Cocaine? Alcohol? No. The two biggest addictive agents were nicotine and *sugar.* For me, I think the best course of action is to stay away from all white powders.

The irony of the verbiage we use in these programs is not lost on me. In A.A., people talk about *sobriety,* while in the food programs, they speak of *abstinence.* Alcoholics are not sober with their drinking, they *abstain.* It's the food people that need to develop a *sober* relationship with the food, because to abstain means to stay away from it entirely.

The most important reason I believe that recovery from food is harder has to do with the pain involved, or more accurately the manner in which the food *delivers* its pain.

If there is anything good to be said about drugs and alcohol, it's that these substances usually manage to slam their victims face down into the pavement (figuratively, but sometimes literally) with the pain they cause. If the addict survives, there is a point – some point – at which he or she usually has some moment of lucidity where the situation becomes obvious. Whether it involves waking up in jail or a hospital or next to someone they don't know (or don't want to know) – they find themselves with a brief period of honesty where they ask themselves *"What the hell am I doing with my life?"*

Food is not so nice.

The pain that food causes isn't the acute type that drugs and alcohol provide, it's the dull chronic type that will allow a person (especially if they are smart) to keep moving the goalposts of acceptability. With each day, and each increasing number on the scale, that which was previously unacceptable becomes acceptable. "I'll never get to 200 pounds!" the person says on Monday. On Tuesday, after looking at 205 on the scale, the same person says "Okay, but no more than 210."

I had a sponsee, Jim, in one of my food programs, who was 580 pounds. The only way we knew what his weight was that each month we would go together to weigh him on a truck scale at the local dump. Jim was as smart a person as I have ever known. If I had a time machine and had gone back to when Jim was 200 pounds in college and told him that someday he would be 580, he would have laughed me out of the room. But people don't go from 200 to 580. They go from 200 to 225, from 225 to 240. And so on... slowly, slowly up.

That's the main problem with food as an addiction. *Food addiction makes you uncomfortable enough to <u>know</u> you should do something about the problem, but not uncomfortable enough to actually be willing to go to any lengths to do something about it.*

By the way... Jim was one of two sponsees I've had in my food programs that didn't make it. He died in a fire because he was too big to get out. I've also known dozens of others over the years that fell victim to this disease. Some died of heart attacks (including 20 year old anorexics), some died of diabetes complications, and all too many died of suicide – just tired of the struggle. That's the difference between some commercial food programs and the one I am in currently: *I'm in the one with the body count.*

The other problem an overeater faces is something of a logic loop. One of the main things the disease of compulsive eating uses against us is our character defects. To get rid of those character defects involves us being abstinent and working the Steps. As a result, there is often some *white knuckling* involved in the early days of abstinence for compulsive eaters. But the pain is worth it.

The real reason, in my opinion, that so many people fall short when trying to work a 12 Step food program is simple: they don't really understand the disease and how it manifests itself in them. If you don't know what you're fighting, how do you fight it?

I'm a systems analyst in my "day job." Systems analyst is the perfect job for the child of an alcoholic. I get to look at businesses and analyze what they're doing wrong and how they could do better. Those skills were what I called on after my last period of slipping with the food. By looking at what I had done wrong, how things could have been different, and what I had misunderstood, I felt I could keep from repeating the mistakes of the past. So far, for the past 19-plus years, I've been successful at that. What this book attempts to do is impart some of that thinking to those who need it.

Who is this book for?

As I mentioned in the Preface, this is not a book for those who have never tried a food program, but for those who have – but failed or had limited success. If any of the description I just wrote about rings true about you, I beg of you to read this book. If you are going to read this book, you need to follow these instructions for it to work for you:

1. Ask yourself: *Am I ready to recover?* Am I willing to throw myself wholeheartedly into it, based on the guarantee that there is recovery if I do so *with no reservations whatsoever*? If you are like me, you've used up your "get out of hell free" cards. I knew after my major slip that I couldn't keep going up and down with my weight. The next one might kill me.

Recovery from this disease is possible, and it's very much like getting recovery from cancer. To battle cancer, doctors use chemo and radiation treatment. Both protocols involve attacking the body in which the cancer resides. As a result, if you only had a small, *my food plan is punishing ↑ eliminating the deadly disease I have - just like radiation ↑ chemo would be eliminating cancer*

limited idea of what cancer was, you'd tell the doctors you didn't want the chemo or radiation, because they're attacking the cells in your body. The treatment, however, is very precisely directed. Yes, it does attack your body and your cells, but only in that it's attacking the bad cells in your body.

That's what this book is all about. It's about explaining how the disease works and how the treatment for it – while sometimes looking punitive to you – is actually only punitive to the disease that infests your body. Hopefully, when you're done, you'll be in remission from this debilitating disease.

2. *Read the entire book.* I tend to get enthused when I start reading a book, but then fizzle out about halfway through. Because of the nature of what I am talking about, the information contained within this book has crucial sections about conquering the disease, but they tend to be spread out evenly throughout its length. The exact sentence you need to read might be in the next to the last chapter. But you'll only know that if you read the book *to the end.*

3. This book contains lots of practical advice on how to stop compulsively eating, but then how to stay stopped. It also talks about how you can change so that you will *want* to stay stopped. If you work a program that feels like you're hanging on by your fingernails, you're not going to be able to do it for very long – in which case, you've just gotten another temporary fix for your problem.

4. This book talks about recovery from the food obsession, and how to keep the obsession away. These methods to get you to stop eating and stay stopped are only the first step. In a way, it's like locking and bolting the front and back doors of your house. It's great if the disease you're trying to keep out only tries to get in via the front and back doors. The problem is that you've left your windows unlocked and wide open! That's what the Steps are about, and the "windows" are the various character defects and inner turmoil driving the "engine" of the disease. If all you do is put down the food, it's only a matter of time before your disease will find another way in – mostly via your character defects.

My mother, who had been a lifelong alcoholic, hadn't had a drink for 35 years when she died. Her spiritual recovery was, in my opinion, limited. However, she had hit a hellacious bottom and didn't have to be around, see, smell or otherwise interact with *they both can hurt, those treatments, but they are, everyday, working so I can have a life*

alcohol. As a result, she never drank again – and this without really working the 12 Steps beyond admitting she was powerless over alcohol. Although she was technically sober, she was not recovered. I don't think those of us that are food addicts are afforded the luxury she had to avoid working the Steps. We _need_ to work all of the Steps and the Tools of Recovery (found in some of the food programs) as well. The same person _will_ eat again and if we don't do the work, we're cooked.

This book attempts to shed light on the disease of compulsive eating and how it manifests itself in peoples' lives. While it says in the A.A. Big Book that "knowledge of our disease alone will not cure us," (and this is absolutely true)... knowledge about the disease couldn't hurt.

Who am I and what makes me qualified to tell you anything?

Whenever I lead a retreat or workshop, I always talk about the progression of my thinking on this subject. After you've been around the 12 Step programs for a while, and seen what works and what doesn't, there's a part of you that thinks "You know, I think I've got something to contribute and maybe I can help people with my thoughts on this subject."

Then you continue to work the Steps and grow as a person. You grow until you get to the point where you think to yourself "Who the hell am I to be telling anybody anything about anything?"

That's pretty much where I am today. I can tell you something: I've made every mistake there is to make in 12 Step food recovery, so think of me as the guy that's walked through the minefield and gotten blown up like Wile E. Coyote a dozen times. My main contribution might just be me pointing to each of the land mines and saying "Watch out for that one, it's a doozy!"

To be serious for a moment, I came into my first 12 Step program for food in 1981 and while I have gone to different programs over the years, I never left recovery. I'd love to say I have over 30 years of back-to-back abstinence, but that isn't my story. About 19 years ago, I was slipping and sliding with the best of them and couldn't get more than a month of abstinence together. Some important things happened to me about that time, which I will talk about later. As a result, however, I've been abstinent for over 19 years (as of this writing) and maintained over a hundred pound weight loss for most of that time. The exact food program in which

I am battling this disease is irrelevant; it's the Steps and recovery that is important.

Numbers are meaningless. A friend of mine in A.A. called his mother in London upon the occasion of his 20th A.A. Birthday. "Mom," he said. "I haven't had a drop of alcohol in 20 years!" There was a pause at the other end, and then her wry reply was "Well... neither has the cat!"

How this book is structured

Like the disease, there is a bit of the "chicken and egg" to recovery from compulsive eating. As they say: "It's not about the food unless it's about the food, then it's ALL about the food until it's not about the food."

We need to work on putting down the food, but also at the same time we need to address the Steps. In this book, we'll also look at "The Tools of Recovery", which exists in O.A. and CEA-HOW (*refer to the appendix for more information on the individual programs*).

First, I think it's important to get to know me better, so I will tell you my story. Unlike the retreats I lead, I'll hold off on the conclusions I have drawn along the way until later.

Next, I'll talk about the actual disease of compulsive eating. Then we'll look at the first three Steps, and talk about the "nuts and bolts" concerning the food and how to put it down. We'll look some more at the "Tools of Recovery", and then continue our journey through the Steps – taking some time along the way to look at the "defects of character" which continue to feed the "engine" of our disease.

Another huge issue for compulsive eaters is sexuality, intimacy and body image – and for those topics, I've dedicated an entire chapter.

Next, we'll look at other "outside issues," and things like swapping addictions and getting outside help.

Your possible slip and how to prevent it will be the next chapter. How do you put up safeguards to keep you from repeating the pattern of slipping you might have had in the past?

Finally, I'll talk about the gifts of the program. After you do all the work, "what's in it for you?," I hope to explain that as well.

Again, to reiterate something I mentioned earlier: please, please, please... take the time to read this book from cover to cover. Don't let it be just another of the many books about food and weight on your bookshelf that you have only partially read.

Chapter 2 – My Story

Psychologists now believe that a predilection towards addiction and alcoholism is hereditary, but I like to joke that when I was born, the doctor announced "We've bred the perfect alcoholic!" This was really not far from the truth.

I was born and raised in the suburbs of New York City, the son of two Irish Catholic alcoholics (*Irish alcoholics? What are the odds?*). My parents divorced when I was one year old, and I spent the majority of my youth shuttling back and forth between the frying pan and the fire.

My mother was a low bottom alcoholic, who had a propensity for "geographical cures." This meant we were constantly moving as she attempted over and over to pull her life together. I remember being in a 12 Step meeting of children of alcoholics once and hearing the speaker say "We moved six times by the time I was in the sixth grade." I snorted and whispered to the person next to me, "Heck, we moved six times *when* I was in the sixth grade!" And that wasn't a joke.

My father, on the other hand, was a functional alcoholic, meaning he never lost a job over drinking. But he was a car salesman, and I don't think _any_ car salesman ever lost a job over drinking. I think at the time it was *de rigueur* for the position.

While my father was able to earn a living, he wasn't much of a father. He had been a bachelor until his mid-thirties and the idea of raising a child – especially by himself – was not exactly a thrilling prospect for him. At various times, for various reasons, I found myself living with him. While he was a functional alcoholic, he was also a functional rageaholic as well.

During a particularly horrendous four to five year period, I lived a life of pure hell. We'd moved from New York to Denver, back to New York, to Florida, back to New York, back to Florida and lots of shuttling around the entire state of New York in the interim. There was only one constant in my life – food.

There is one enduring fact of life in the U.S. then and now – no matter where you go, you can find junk food. I think if you scale Mt. Rainier, you can find Twinkies at the top somewhere.

Thank God for food.

Food was the only thing that coated incredibly raw nerves. Food was there when the police showed up and told me my mother was in jail. Food was there when she was in rehab, or missing for days at a time. While it became my curse later in life, it kept me alive long enough to find help.

A wise old-timer who runs a large A.A. group in Los Angeles says "Some people just need to drink. It keeps them alive. We can't sober up a corpse." This was the case with me. I truly think if things had gotten just a *little* worse – or I didn't have the food – I might have killed myself.

Along with the propensity for alcohol that got passed down from both sides of the family (there are horror stories from generations past that I will spare you here), I got all of the bad attitudes and skewed world view that only a family of alcoholics can pass down to their children.

When I look back at my parents at the time I was growing up, I realize I was being raised by two people who were, in terms of their emotional growth, children. I wish I could at least equate their emotional maturity to that of teenagers, but children was really more the truth. As a result, I see now that I shouldn't have expected to grow emotionally anywhere past that level without outside help. If you are taught to play tennis by a lousy tennis player, chances are you'll never get any better than a lousy tennis player. To get better, you need to start working with better tennis players. Emotional children tend to raise emotional children and to quote an Al Anon phrase: *hurt people hurt people.*

While I am talking about my story, which includes alcoholic parents, I have heard this story from other people in program whose parents never touched a drop. Those parents, however, were compulsive eaters, or narcissists or had some other dysfunction that left them in the same situation. The specifics about alcohol are secondary – as is, I believe – the choice of substance that people later abuse. Food, drugs, alcohol, gambling, sex – pick your poison or bad behavior – it's still about finding a way to run away from scary emotions.

The dysfunctional way my family dealt with their feelings and emotions was simple – they chose to not deal with them at all. Neither of my parents had very much access to emotions. My mother had shut down her emotions early in life dealing with a tyrannical father. My father for reasons I still don't understand was the same.

While there was lots of talking in our household, we never talked about feelings. We would talk about politics, baseball, or how "da bastards" were screwing us over. "Da bastards" is the generic term for whomever either of my parents felt were responsible for all of their problems on any given day – *never themselves, of course.*

The last thing alcoholics want to talk about is their feelings, especially if they are *uncomfortable* feelings. You can almost hear the "beep-beep-beep" as they back away from them. At the end of what turned out to be the last face-to-face meeting of my brother and my mother, my brother started to get emotional. This was not an irrational thing as she was old and frail and he lived a continent away and probably wouldn't see her again (and didn't). As soon as his voice started to crack, she interrupted with "Well, don't worry, we'll see each other again, all is well."

Her abrupt need to change the subject and stop the emotion – even if it was someone else's emotion – was typical in my family. Let's do anything to not have to deal with an uncomfortable emotion. Is it any wonder children of such people end up abusing some kind of substance or process?

The most important message I got growing up was something never _said_ to me, but something imparted to me on a subconscious level. When a child watches a parent go through some kind of emotional turmoil, then immediately say "I *need* a ..." (drink, cigarette, pill, something/anything), it sends a very strong message to an impressionable child. It says: *"If I don't like the way I'm feeling, there's something outside me that I can put inside me that will make things better."*

I learned this lesson well.

I have joked that as a kid I found food because they hadn't invented crack yet. I needed food because despite all of the crazy things going on around me, when I ate – I got calmer. I think one of the things I needed to do when looking back at my history with food was to acknowledge it did something for me; I was self-medicating. Otherwise, I wouldn't have used it. I wasn't dumb!

The further problem with my life-long love/hate relationship with food was that, while food was effective at first, it came with a raft of side-effects, most notably weight gain. Sadly, food's soothing effects slowly ebbed away to the point it wasn't doing anything for me at the end, but it was all I knew how to do.

The first man in O.A. was a gentleman named A.G. and he used to say "There's no hell on Earth like being a fat kid." I can certainly attest to that. I've been a fat kid and a fat adult and being a fat kid is a whole lot worse. Kids can be brutal and often were. I was almost constantly bullied from about the fourth grade onwards.

When you're a fat kid that feels like garbage about your body, you want to grasp onto any thin straw of self-esteem you can find. For me, that was my brain. I was a "gifted child" who escaped in reading and learning. Even this gift had its cost because it estranged me even further from my peers. Until I was sober a few years, I rarely missed an opportunity to let people know just how smart I was. It was the only way I ever felt good about myself. Not only was I different because I was "the whale," I was the kid who messed everything up when they graded on the curve. With a childhood like that, is it any wonder that I always felt different? There was the world and then there was John.

At the age of thirteen, my mother's drinking got so bad, I was sent to live permanently with my father. My father and I couldn't have been more different. From the time I moved back with him until I moved out on my own, we were barely on speaking terms.

For years I thought my father was the cause of most of my problems. Truthfully though, I didn't like him whether he was drunk or sober. It took years of therapy to realize it was my mother who caused me the most problems. This was because of the inconsistency that came from her drinking. When she was sober, she was a great mother – funny and smart. She gave me my sense of humor, and my warped way of looking at the world. When she was drunk however, she was horrible. I often hear people talk about living in a "*Dr. Jekyll and Mr. Hyde*" household, which I find humorous. Robert Louis Stevenson wrote that story as an allegory about alcoholism.

I went to High School in Greenwich, Connecticut, a very affluent town on the east coast of the United States. However, my father was a car salesman – with a car salesman's income – and we lived in a one room apartment. I was not even able to afford a bicycle to get to school. Meanwhile other kids were driving up in

Mercedes. Like I'm not feeling "less than" enough about being the fat kid, now I'm the *poor* fat kid!

At that time in my life, it was all about my weight. I knew I needed – and desperately wanted – to lose weight. I tried every diet and I was the only male in a Weight Watchers meeting when I was 13 years old. I was surrounded by "old ladies" (who were probably 30 – I wish I were that "old" again). Like many eaters, I also had a closet full of all sizes of clothes, most of which were too small for me. I heard someone once call those small clothes in your closet "aspirational clothing."

When I was new to 12 Step programs, I used to say that none of the diets ever worked for me. In retrospect, that was not true – they *all* worked. *Once*. I would get excited about the diet, study it, and then follow it exactly as if it were the Holy Grail. Because I'm a good student and can follow a syllabus, I would quit the debating society and do as I was told – and I would start to lose weight. The trouble is that I have a disease called compulsive overeating. It affects my decision making process. As soon as I gave my broken brain permission to give input, I would start looking for the loopholes and it wasn't long before those loopholes tore through the whole fabric of the diet. I had allowed the brain of a compulsive eater to begin making the decisions again about the food, and that *never* ends well. The result was, of course, that I would gain all of the weight back – and then some. As a friend put it once: "Looking back I didn't go on a diet – I just sent my weight out for reinforcements."

Back in high school, I soon found my niche – with all the other "weirdoes." The smarter you are, the more convoluted you need to make the head games you play with yourself. I *knew* I was different (less than), and that I couldn't possibly hold up well to any comparison with a *real* person. So I would take the initiative. It was the seventies and while everyone was wearing jeans to school, I'd show up in a starched shirt and a tie. I would tell myself that my peers – who professed to be rebelling against "the establishment" were actually just rebuilding it in their own image. Lemmings, I would call them. The truth was, however, that I felt totally alien. So why not go out of the way to be different and convince yourself it was *your* idea?

So I continued through high school: not going out on any dates, not going to the prom, mostly hanging out with the other social outcasts. In my alone times, I would go into my classic eating mode: sweet/salt/sweet/salt. All the time I wondered why I could not lose weight. And I'm supposed to be smart.

I deliberately didn't drink during High School, which was not easy as Greenwich High was a party school. Being the brainiac that I was, I had read about children of alcoholics. All of the literature said that many children of alcoholics tend to grow up to become alcoholics themselves. Well that was the last thing I wanted, to turn out like my parents!

Still, I was a teenager driven by hormones. I had a crush on a girl that I desperately wanted to get to know better. We both worked at the local Woolworth's and she invited me to go out drinking after work with her and her friends. I agreed to go, and immediately panic set in. I was – and to a certain extent still am – uncomfortable in social situations. Add to that the fact that I wanted to *somehow* make a good impression on this girl I had a crush on. Then to top it off, there was the peer pressure that everyone else was drinking and well... the rest was history.

Once I had a drink I started to calm down, and then another. I got even calmer and the knot in my stomach started to go away. What I hadn't realized was that the years of psychological turmoil had me walking around with a constant knot in my stomach. Alcohol made that knot go away. I look back now with a little recovery and sanity and think: *who wouldn't want to lose a constant knot in their stomach?* Most people walked around *without* a knot in their stomach, but I didn't know that. It never occurred to me that there was something wrong with my thinking in general that caused me to *have* that knot. All that thinking was irrelevant, because I had found the answer – and it was in a bottle.

So I was able to talk to that girl and she invited me to go out with her crowd again on Saturday, which I did as well. Then she said, "Well, this is what we do – we go out Friday and Saturday night." My immediate thought was, "Well, if Friday and Saturday are good, then Friday, Saturday, Sunday, Monday, Tuesday, Wednesday and Thursday would be just that much better!" *(Addicts have no concept of diminishing returns.)*

Within a short time I was drinking on a regular basis. For the first time in my life, I was able to lose weight! I know now this was because I had simply changed my sugar intake from solid to liquid. Somehow, I instinctively knew I had no real control over my food, so I lost weight in the only manner that worked for me at that time: not eating. I would fast for the better part of a week, have a binge, then drink and start the whole thing over again the next week. Add to that a good dose of compulsive exercising and even compulsive eaters can lose weight – *temporarily*. Moderation was a foreign word to me.

I would go running at night and would run to such an extent that I passed out along the side of the road more than once. I find it interesting when people talking about our disease as being one of "lack of willpower." I remember these running episodes and think "Damn! That takes a lot of willpower!" And it did. I would run for 5 or more miles and never enjoyed a minute of it (I later came to enjoy exercising). Despite that, I would run until I passed out, wanting to stop at every step. But with the food? No such luck. I know now that's not a lack of willpower, that's a disease.

I got down to a normal weight for the first time in my life, and stayed there for about 10 seconds. Except now, I am a crazy lunatic drunk, and very soon the alcohol took over my life. There's a saying in A.A. that also applies to an extent with food: "The man takes the drink, then the drink takes the drink, and then the drink takes the man." Soon, even though I had my first girlfriend, the alcohol became more important to me than she was.

Very quickly into my drinking, by the way, the food reappeared. I also describe my life cycle with my addictions this way: I was fat, then I was a drunk, then I was a fat drunk. My alcoholism went zero to sixty in no time and even though I only drank for seven years, I had my lifetime supply of alcohol.

I had my fill of crazy stories of waking up places not knowing how I got there. I have more than one story of finding myself on my back on the floor of a bar with a guy with a pool cue standing over me. This was because even though I was not a physical person, I was a very angry person and I displayed it with razor sharp sarcasm that I wielded with the deftness of a great executioner. Unfortunately, I used it on people holding pool cues who replied by beating me senseless.

In December of 1980, John Lennon was shot and it reinforced my dismal view of the world. So I drank myself into oblivion from then (December 8th) until Christmas week, when I checked into an alcohol detox in Norwalk, CT. At the time I entered, I was vomiting blood, was having auditory hallucinations, and would occasionally lose the feeling in my right arm, thanks to alcoholic neuritis.

They preached 12 Step recovery at the detox. I was familiar with it because I had gone to meetings with my mother as a kid (they had great donuts), and had even attended a couple of meetings in the months leading up to my institutionalization. I wanted nothing to do with 12 Step recovery. To me, 12 Step programs were religious organizations. Since I was a stone cold atheist, a religious organization wasn't going to work for me.

To illustrate how arrogant and unteachable I was, I got thrown out of the detox. Do you know how demoralizing it is to be kicked out of a detox? So I went and did what most people newly out of detox do: I got drunk again (*I'll show them*)!

The next morning however, something shifted in me. It was a Sunday, I got up and went to a meeting (one of the ones they had been bringing us to while in detox). After the meeting, I started talking to a guy while putting away chairs. I told him I didn't think I was an alcoholic because I stopped for a few weeks a couple months back, and for a whole month the year before. He pointed out that people who _aren't_ alcoholics don't have to stop drinking periodically to prove to themselves that they're not alcoholics. Yikes – busted.

I went on to say that I couldn't be part of a religious program. "It's not a religious program, it's a spiritual program," he responded. I continued to argue with him, pointing to all of the places in the Steps where it said "God" or "Him."

He stood there for a moment with a wry smile and then said "Okay, leave it out."

I stared at him like a robot that had been put into some kind of a loop. What the heck did he mean "*leave it out?*"

"Right now, your disease is looking for any reason to head out that door," he said to me. "What could be better than the excuse that this program is going to push some religion on you? So just leave it out. You can live sober working the 12 Steps for the rest of your life and nobody will _ever_ tell you what to believe or that you have to believe."

I had a spiritual awakening of a kind at that moment. Suddenly, all of the intellectual fight went out of me. His words and reasoning were brilliant. Had he said, as I've heard some old timers tell newcomers about the spiritual side, "_Keep coming back, you'll get it._" I would have run out of the door thinking, "Oh my God, this _cult_ is going to get me."

The fact that he told me I didn't have to believe _anything_ that I could come to believe _or not believe_ as I saw fit caused the small mustard seed of understanding I needed to be planted.

As I began my alcohol recovery, I was at my top weight, almost 300 pounds. I immediately began trying to lose weight the way I had earlier – by fasting and drastic exercise. Like many newly recovered people, moderation was not in my vocabulary. By then, I had heard vaguely about Overeaters Anonymous and other 12 Step food programs and knew it was something I should check out, but I didn't.

It was around this time that I found I was able to purge and this was, in my eyes, a boon to my ability to lose weight. If I could fast until I couldn't take the hunger any more, then binged, I had a way to handle that binge! Brilliant!

After I was sober for a while, I had a slip and didn't tell anybody. Then I drank again and didn't say anything. Then again. Eventually I came to see that the only way that cycle was going to stop involved me fessing up and starting my sobriety over again. I did and that was on October 17, 1981. As of this writing, I have not had the need to drink alcohol since.

By that time, I knew I needed to address my lifelong compulsive eating problem. I went to my sponsor and said "I need to get help for my food addiction." This isn't what an alcohol sponsor wants to hear from someone with a few days of sobriety. In fact, the common thing to say to a newcomer is "Here, have a donut!" I explained to my sponsor that my two diseases were working _together_ and that I had been an eater long before I was a drinker. Finally, he said to me, "Okay, as long as you go to the meetings I want you to attend I don't care what you do over and above that." It was a deal. I walked into my first meeting of a 12 Step food program within a few days of my sobriety date.

I knew I was home from the first meeting. Everything that was said about the disease made so much sense, and answered so many questions about why I couldn't get ahead of the eating problem.

I threw myself headlong into both programs. I got a food sponsor, and most importantly to me at that time, I found a food plan pamphlet and chose a diet. If there is one thing I knew how to do, it was follow a diet. The added thing was I now understood – actually believed to the core of my soul – that I was a compulsive overeater. I would need to abstain from compulsive eating, one day at a time, for the rest of my life.

Being a 26 year old male and with the metabolism of a hummingbird (I would kill for that metabolism now, by the way), I lost weight very fast. Soon afterwards, my first food sponsor left program and I decided I really didn't need another food sponsor. After all, I had one in the other program and I didn't need two. (What I didn't realize then was that this is not a home-study program. I didn't know that then, but my subsequent failure made it tragically obvious.)

In looking back, the main reason I didn't want a sponsor was because I didn't want to be _accountable_ for my food choices and actions to another person. I didn't want to have to tell someone what I'm eating and I certainly didn't want to tell someone when I screwed up!

In my early days in that program, for the one and only time in my life, I was anorexic. This is an interesting story that I will go into more depth on in the chapter on sexuality and body image. The upshot was that I had been every iteration of an eating disorder: a compulsive overeater, bulimic, exercise bulimic and anorexic. Look up the phrase compulsive overeater and I think my picture is there. I was *"thin is not well"* on the hoof.

While I began to recover, I started dabbling with a new career. I had been working at a magazine in Westport, CT during the day. It was the early eighties and the comedy club boom had begun. I started exploring my ability to do standup comedy, and within a short time I was getting work all over New England. Suddenly, between the job during the day and the comedy at night, I had no time for meetings in *both* programs.

Well, that really wasn't a problem. I knew what I had to do. I truly understood that I was a compulsive overeater, and as long as

I had my trusty food plan, I'd be okay. "Four ounces of chicken is the answer to all my problems today" became my slogan.

The patience of the disease is amazing. After staying abstinent for a year or so without many meetings, I figured I had the disease under control. So one night after a show at Dangerfield's in New York City, someone suggested we go down to Chinatown for a late night snack. Sounded like a good idea to me. Then again putting whiskey into a glass of milk seemed like a good idea to the guy talked about in the Big Book (if you haven't read that story, you should – just start at the beginning and read until you find it).

To make a short story even shorter, within a few days I was back in the food. I got to know every Korean grocer between the Eastside comedy clubs and the highway. I nicknamed my car "Meals on Wheels." Before I stopped drinking, if I took a turn too hard, you could hear the clink of bottles under my seat. Now you could hear the crinkle of cellophane.

I found myself defeated again. Now I had to drag my fat butt and overloaded ego back to program. That was hard. I had been so arrogant the first time around. "Why can't these people get it?" I would ask scornfully. Now I was one of "those people." Pitiful and incomprehensible demoralization was putting it mildly. Little did I know (because I hadn't picked up the Big Book very much) that my story echoed that of "Bill's Story." Both of us had come to accept our disease, knew we had to handle it, and yet we had both fallen flat on our faces despite our *"vast intelligence."* I would have termed it "humbling," if I knew what that word meant at that time.

So I came back to program. I would get a few days of abstinence, and then slip. Then I would get another week and *plop* – on my face again. That cycle went on for quite a while.

Every once in a while, a thought comes into my head from so far out in left field – saying something that shocks even me – that I can't help feel it's the voice of my Higher Power. "Why doesn't it work now liked it did the first time?" was what I had asked, and the answer came back: *"Maybe you didn't do it right the first time."*

That was exactly what the problem was. I had lived through a classic food recovery story. I believe a lot of people get that one "grace" abstinence where the Abstinence Fairy hits you on the head with the wand and poof! You're abstinent. You can mess it up six ways from Sunday, but it still works. The trouble was that because it was _so_ easy and effortless, it seemed logical that it would be easy to get back. I believe this is the reason that some people like myself who have a "pink cloud" abstinence the first time invariably throw it away at some point. The sad thing is that many then spend years trying to chase that "pink cloud" dream of easy recovery. In my experience, if you were gifted with that type of instant recovery, hold onto it. You won't get another one, and the second one is a _lot_ more work as a result.

I realized that my first go around with the food program was exactly the same as the first go around with all of the other diets I had done over the years. I had followed direction, I had gotten out of the way and it worked. The second time around, however, my diseased brain was trying to run the show again. Also, I wanted to do it the way I had before, without a sponsor, and without doing any of the other work.

"I've got to do this by the book," I thought to myself. "What did I do that worked in getting sober?" I asked myself. The answer was that then I was willing to do whatever they wanted me to do. Tell me to strip naked and stand out on the corner and I'd ask "What time?"

I regained my abstinence and things were pretty good for a number of years. I met a woman, we got married, and my standup career flourished. I played clubs in almost every town east of the Mississippi. I wanted to move to L.A. to pursue a writing career, and so we eventually did. While such a move can be traumatic, my abstinence held pretty steady during those first early days in L.A. However, as time went on, the food started to take control again. Within a short while, I was in "the cycle from hell."

My vision of this "cycle from hell" is like that of a loop. I would start thinking about the food, but hold on with white knuckles to my abstinence. Then I would break my abstinence and get into the food. Then I would start trying to get abstinent again until I would finally get it back. Then I would obsess on losing the weight I had gained during my time "out." When I finally got the weight off and all was starting to get "quiet" again, I would start the cycle all over again.

They say "_program ruins your eating_" and I can attest to that. First, you remember how you felt when you were abstinent. You felt good physically, and you felt good about yourself mentally as well. When you get back in the food and it reaches the point where you're feeling guilty even *before* you've taken the first bite, your compulsive eating is indeed ruined. When that happened to me, I remember wondering why I was even doing it. It was simply that eating was the only way I knew how to deal with the deeply embedded emotional turmoil in me. That turmoil was so deep I couldn't even recognize there *was* turmoil.

All of this was happening to a person who by now had 15 years in the program! I was trying to do all the things they taught me to do: I had a sponsor, I was sponsoring, had service commitments, and was even an Intergroup Delegate! Yet, when I finished the night as secretary of one of my meetings, I'd stop at the donut shop on the way home. I remember thinking "This is crazy, John. You're not sentenced to O.A. If you want to eat, go eat!" Therein lays that underlying fact: I *didn't* want to eat, but I couldn't stop either.

Finally, it got bad enough that I started attending meetings of another 12 Step fellowship that was much stricter about the food. I knew this was what I needed to do, because I just couldn't stop. Getting that abstinence took a while, as I would get about four days of abstinence and then the sugar/flour withdrawal was too much and I would eat. Finally, one week I did something I had heard about for years, but never tried firsthand: I decided to take it *one day at a time*! It was Friday night and I was at my usual four day mark (you always restart on Monday, right?) and I was climbing the walls. At that point, I gave myself permission to eat whatever I wanted, as much as I wanted... *tomorrow morning*. I also asked for help from my Higher Power, something I rarely, if ever, did. After I awoke and had an abstinent breakfast, I told myself, if I still wanted to eat I could dig in.

Lo and behold, the thing I had been telling my sponsees for years actually worked for me. The "withdrawal fever" broke and I started this long, sustained abstinence.

I also knew something was driving me to eat, and I needed to get to the bottom of it, so I got back into therapy. As it says in the program literature, "we are not professionals," and while I trusted my new sponsor, I knew I needed outside help. The great line from program was all too true in my case: "*If you want to find out why you're eating... stop eating!*"

After months of both abstinence and therapy, something arose that was right in front of my eyes, but buried deep down: *I was in a marriage I didn't want to be in.* While I had deep affection for my wife, I didn't feel what I thought other people did, and I doubt I ever had. The trouble was that I was a people pleaser and the idea of having to go to a woman who loved me and tell her I didn't love her was beyond painful. I'd rather do almost anything than that... *like eat.*

In my warped brain, as much as I said I was powerless over the food, I really didn't believe it. In my head, if things got bad, I could turn to the food and while it was painful as well, it was something I had convinced myself I could turn on and off – *when I was ready.*

Looking back in the years since I regained my abstinence, I saw what changed. I have done lots more Step work on myself than I had in all the previous years. I was able to look back and try to understand "what went wrong." I began to see more and more how the disease could wheedle its way back in to a person's life – even one who was well aware of (or thought he was aware of) how the disease worked.

This story, I believe, has a happy ending.

The divorce from my first wife was painful to both of us at the time, however we have since become friends. She went on to marry a terrific guy, and they both ended up in the same program I attend to this day.

On my side of the story, I met and later married a wonderful woman with whom I plan on spending the rest of my life. We are happy, true partners, and have a life – as was said by the founder of O.A. – *"beyond our wildest dreams."*

Hopefully, this book will help you achieve the same gifts I have been given. Through the recovery that came from a lot of hard work, I'm a better person today. I'm relatively serene, have food in its rightful place, and seem able to weather with grace anything life has to offer.

I hope this book can impart to you some of what I had to learn the hard way. If I can help you avoid some of the pitfalls I encountered, this endeavor will have been a success.

If a 12 Step food program can work for me: a cynical, arrogant, and oppositional alcoholic and compulsive eater, it can surely work for you.

Chapter 3 – Step 1: Waving the white flag

Believing It IS a disease and that it is HARD

In looking back on why it took me so long to get long term abstinence, I realize it was partly due to my inability to "get" that compulsive eating is truly a disease. I would go to meetings and my lips would say "disease" whenever I talked about it, but did I *really* believe it? In retrospect, I did not.

I think there was part of me that "bought" the concept, but there was another part that never wanted to look at it too closely, lest my belief in the 12 Steps dissolve before my eyes. If it wasn't a disease, then what the heck was it? In the back of my head, I think my thoughts were: "If you folks want to call it a disease, and it makes you feel better, then fine – call it a disease."

It wasn't until much later that I came to believe it was a disease. What led me to that different conclusion took further analysis of the disease after my own horrendous slip.

Firstly, like all other diseases, none of us ever asked for this. Given everything I have seen and heard over the years, I don't think there is one person who – if he/she had their druthers – would choose to be a compulsive eater. Secondly, the symptoms of this disease are easily identifiable and uniform across all social strata. When I go to my home meeting here in L.A., I can hear an ex-gang member from South Central one week, and a rich Beverly Hills housewife the next, and they tell the exact same story! The details are different, the food might be different, but I hear the same pitiful and incomprehensible demoralization from everyone. Plus it's never an upward trending story – until recovery.

Is compulsive overeating a disease in the standard thinking? A disease is a pathological condition that affects part of an organism. Using that definition, can we identify the disease's cause and effect scientifically? My answer is *"not yet."* To say that we never will would be folly. I truly believe it will only be a matter of time before scientists come to isolate some physiological aspects of this disease, just like they have done with alcohol.

When the A.A. Big Book was written, the writers spoke of how certain drinkers passed that "invisible line" where their ability to have a choice about stopping – once drinking had started – was erased. Scientists have, in recent years, found an enzyme called alcohol dehydrogenase that has been shown to have a significant role in alcoholism and the body's ability to metabolize alcohol. The point is that often science lags behind that which is already commonly known to those who suffer from the disease.

Let's think about the concept of disease for a moment. People get cancer, which is considered a disease – but is it really some foreign thing? No. In the case of cancer, it's an abnormal growth rate in cells. Other diseases have other abnormalities, yet they exist _within_ the body of the sufferer. In other words, people suffering from cancer are growing those cells themselves. Nobody however, considers that they want it and wouldn't choose to not have those cells reproducing if they had a choice in it.

In the case of compulsive eating, the disease affects how our brains function with respect to food. Because it's in our brains – and because we can't (yet) show a picture of bad cells, it's easy to dismiss the concept of it being a disease. Instead, we think of compulsive eating as something we _decided_ to do after previously deciding to _not_ do it. If we suffered from epilepsy, another brain disease, we wouldn't feel guilty about having a seizure, because that's one of the symptoms of epilepsy. Often we do feel guilty about giving in to the food, not realizing _we_ didn't give into the food, _the disease_ forced us to give into the food. The main reason we do "give in" is because we don't recognize where we stop and the disease begins.

I always like to say that the disease of compulsive eating is like the world's best salesman. Imagine a salesman who is the most charming, likable person – who also is the smoothest talker on the planet. Now imagine he is selling something that you had really liked at one time in your life, but decided was no longer good for you. That salesman already has a half a foot in the door, doesn't he? Now imagine that this salesman can also _read your mind_. Whatever you're going to say to decline the offer, he has a logical counter argument all ready to go. Imagine how hard it would be to say "no" to that salesman. _That's the disease of compulsive eating._

Now here's the nastiest part of that salesman's "pitch": when he's done, and he's "made the sale" and you've picked up the food, he leans over and whispers in your ear: *"remember, this was your idea all along."*

But was it *really* your idea? If it was, would you be going to all those meetings? Why would you be doing all the work to try to stay abstinent? Of course it wasn't your idea, *it was the disease's idea.* At the exact moment of deciding to eat, the disease won the day and made the sale. In my opinion, the reason the disease wins and makes the sale so often is that people don't really understand the concept of addiction and the disease of compulsive eating.

What is addiction anyway? To me, the main indicator is when a person decides to do (or not do) something and then goes against that decision – over and over again. When I first moved to L.A., I started getting the local newspaper so that I could be better acclimated to what was going on in the area. After a few years, however, I decided I had read all I needed to and was now just killing trees. So I called the newspaper and cancelled my subscription. Do you know what I did NOT do? I didn't call up the next day and ask for the deliveries to start again – and re-cancel the subscription the day after that. In fact I have never done that kind of activity with anything except the substances to which I was addicted. How about you?

What this book will (hopefully) do is help you to see how to deal with your disease. And for that, knowledge is the key.

Suppose you were diagnosed with cancer, but knew little about it. Then the doctor comes to you and says "We're going to inject some poisonous chemicals into you that will make you very sick. Then we're going to give you radiation treatment which is also not very good for you. Both of these will kill a lot of living cells in your body."

The normal reaction to that would be: no way! That's because the doctor hadn't yet explained to you that both the chemo and the radiation, while attacking the cells in your body, are mostly attacking the cancer cells in your body. The trouble with all diseases is that the bad cells often live right alongside the good cells. This is also the case with compulsive eating. The part of my brain that tells me I need to go eat lots of food when I am having bad feelings resides right along the other cells in my brain that have provided me lots of good thinking in my life. The "little voice" that tells me to go eat sounds just like the voice that told me a second ago where to turn left on the way to the store. What I need to do is listen for _what_ that voice is saying to me rather than how it sounds.

As I mentioned in Chapter 1, one of the keys to this disease is acknowledging how hard it can be to find long term recovery. The pain the food delivers is that dull, chronic pain that a person can get used to – even if the person doesn't like it.

Scientists found out a long time ago that if you take a living frog and bring it toward boiling water, it will thrash to try to move away from it. It's not dumb, and realizes that boiling water is not its friend. However, scientists realized that if you put that same frog into a pot of room temperature water and slowly bring up the temperature, that frog will never jump out of the pot. It will die in that pot of boiling water – the same pot it would have never jumped in. In what kind of pots of boiling water are we stewing – as we grow bigger and bigger?

The boiling water story is the perfect analogy for the food. A slow, gradual slide that – if you're smart enough – you can adjust to faster than it brings you down. For instance, you set a goal on the scale ("If I ever get to 200 pounds I'll really get serious about losing weight!"). After you hit that number (and pass it), a while later you adjust that magic number upwards. Or you start wearing elastic waist clothes and always look at yourself in the mirror from the neck up. Onward and onward – or rather downward and downward.

This is a deadly disease. A friend of mine's mother died of cirrhosis of the liver. Her mother rarely drank alcohol, but she was a compulsive eater that ate a lot of sugar. The liver converts sugar into fat and that can turn into a fatty liver and then later into cirrhosis. You can develop insulin resistance, a precursor to Diabetes Type 2, and then later Diabetes itself. People who die from Diabetes often die on the installment plan – losing limbs, their eyesight, and more. Severely overweight people get heart disease and cancers at a much higher rate than thin people. Why? Insulin promotes tumor growth and inflammatory disease.

Chances are, though, you know all this already. Fear of death doesn't scare a lot of us. Well, it might scare us, but the disease just has too strong a hold. To be honest, if you're seriously into the food, you're already on the downward slide toward death already. That death might not be a physical death, but certainly a mental and spiritual death.

As a good friend who leads O.A. retreats says: *"I'm not afraid of dying from this disease, but of becoming one of the walking dead."* By that he means becoming the kind of person whose whole life is getting up, going to work, coming home, sitting in front of the TV and eating all night (or surfing the net). Then going to bed, sleeping and getting up in the morning and starting the cycle all over again. They are never going out and living, doing any of the limitless things life has to offer. These people, on their deathbed, will be asking themselves what they had done for the last years of their lives.

For me, there has to be more to life than that. No food is worth that kind of life.

What is the disease and how does it manifest itself?

The nature of addiction is that it will constantly tell you that you're in control when you are – in actuality – not in control at all. For a few years before I came into A.A., I would say to myself "I can quit whenever I want to, I just don't want to!" *Right...*

How many times have I had sponsees say to me, "I ate because"... and I stop them right there. I'm sure the reason they are about to expound upon is a perfectly understandable one. The truth is much simpler, I tell them: "You ate because you are a compulsive overeater! Think about it for a moment. Whatever it is you have as the excuse... did it make you want to run out and place a bet? No! Why? Because you're not a compulsive gambler!"

Like alcoholism, compulsive eating runs in families. When you've had the disease of compulsive eating your whole life, and you are surrounded by other compulsive eaters, you lose sight of the fact that other people don't react to troubling incidents, emotional anguish, or even elation with food.

Also, intelligence has little to do with it. I'm a pretty smart guy, but when it came to my disease, I might as well have been a newborn babe. That's the strange paradox of the disease: often the smarter you are, the easier it is to convince yourself that you'll figure out the solution. As is said in program, "there's nobody too dumb to find recovery, but there are a lot of people too smart." Also, the more you know about the disease, the more convoluted the head games have to get. Since I knew a lot about the disease – especially after I had been around the program for a while – the reasoning for my eating became downright labyrinthine.

That... right there... that type of thinking _is_ the disease!

One of the most important shifts came for me when I started being able to see the disease in a different way. _I needed to start seeing it almost like an enemy attacking me._ Otherwise, what was my reasoning? One day I make a decision to do something and the next I change my mind? Then the day after that I revert to my original thinking and the day after that back again? _That's insanity._

The disease is also a lot like "The Andromeda Strain." In that book (and film), the disease was one that was constantly mutating, making it incredibly hard for the people trying to fight it to pin it down. The same is true with compulsive eating. In the beginning, the voice of the disease is often very recognizable. It might say something like "Hey, let's go to the local 7-Eleven and buy a bunch of binge food and eat it!"

After some time of being abstinent, however, that sales pitch would fall on deaf ears. The disease – always the consummate salesman – works very hard to figure out how to "get a foot in the door." It then backs up, and backs up, and backs up until it can find a chink in the armor of a compulsive eater. Since the disease knows a frontal assault is out of the question, it falls back to something like: "_You know... you're going to too many meetings._" If that works, it's done the job it set out to do: it has nudged you just slightly off the right path. It's like what scientists have figured out about a possible meteor heading toward Earth: they don't have to blow it up, they just have to go far enough out and then just nudge it a little. If you nudge something just a little, but you do it far enough away, by the time it travels a long distance it is way off course.

As I said earlier in _"Why is recovery from food addiction so hard?"_, food has many more ways to attack us than any of the other addictive substances. The other thing is that if we have something of a flexible food plan, we have to be willing to be doubly careful. One of the founding fathers of the United States once said "The price of liberty is eternal vigilance." The same is true for abstinence.

While this amorphous blob called "the disease" is hard to pin down, we can identify some of the discrete signs and symptoms.

The Big Book talks about the overall definition in the simple way that most people have heard. The book talks about "an allergy of the body and obsession of the mind." To put it another way, "the inability to stop once started, and the inability to keep from starting again." As with most things in the Big Book, it is a simple elegant explanation of the overall "strategy" of our disease. It's also important to then look more granularly at the disease's "attack plan."

Honesty: First and foremost, my disease wraps itself around the honesty center of the brain. I'm not talking about "checkbook honesty," most of us pride ourselves on that kind of honesty. But what about honesty when it is concerning our food? Not so much. While I'm often not too honest about my food with others when I'm in the food, I am mostly dishonest with myself. I have an almost unlimited amount of self-delusion when it comes to food – and that is not me, but my disease hard at work to convince me that "everything is fine." As long as I think things are fine, I haven't taken the first Step in admitting I have a problem. If I don't have a problem, I don't have to look for a solution.

If I am trying to get abstinent, the disease has only one job to do every day: to get me to put off dealing with the food for another day. This is smart thinking on my disease's part: if it can convince me to put off recovery just one more day... then that's one more day it's got the foot in the door. Chances are if it can convince me to delay recovery today, it will be able to convince me again tomorrow as well. Reciting the "tomorrow mantra" was responsible for years of delayed recovery for me.

The "tomorrow mantra" is strong – and it's part and parcel of the illusion of power*ful*ness. Can I start today? No, it's not a Monday, or the first of the month, or... not now – we've just entered the holiday season. For eaters, the "holiday season" is bookended by the two candy holidays: Halloween and Valentine's Day. There's one indisputable fact: if you are in a room full of recovering compulsive eaters, *none of them started their abstinence on a tomorrow.* They all started it on a *today.* The main difference between the people with long term abstinence and those without it was that at some point in their first week of abstinence, when they were ready to say "Screw it, what's another day or two?" they found the _power_ to fight that thought, recognizing it as the voice of their disease. For me, that _power_ was not of my own doing. It came from some kind of a Higher Power that decided that I had had enough. That was something, however, I didn't realize until years later.

My disease is cunning, baffling and powerful and will try anything it can to keep me from taking action on stopping the addiction cycle. The maddening thing about this disease is that there is no getting ahead of it. Everything I learn about this disease is simply more ammunition for it to use against me. Having heard someone at a meeting who was also battling the disease say "I'm praying for the willingness" was all I needed (or should I say all my disease needed) to latch onto. There is, of course, nothing wrong with many of the program phrases you hear, but an active disease can grab onto those phrases, twist them around, and come up with a reason – using those phrases – why I should go another day without putting down the food.

This happened for me when I was trying to get my abstinence back in a program with a flexible food plan. I would come to meetings, hoping to be inspired. If truth be told, I was coming to meetings hoping that the "Abstinence Fairy" would come back and give me back that first grace abstinence that was easy and brought no urges with it. In other words, I wanted what everyone had without doing any of the work. That kind of thinking is another aspect of the disease, and another weapon in my disease's arsenal.

I particularly used that tired old saw "I'm praying for the willingness." As I said earlier, w_hen it comes to addiction, willingness is highly overrated._ Of course, the reality is that we all need to be willing in order to recover. At that exact point in time, however, my disease was trying to use the program concept of willingness _against me_ as a way to get me to "kick the can down the road" another day when it came to actually putting down the food. That phrase also did double duty for me. Not only did it keep me from actually putting down the food, but it also made me feel like I was actually doing something when indeed I was not. I had just come to use a program phrase to justify my continued eating.

"A little knowledge can be dangerous" was the story of my relapse. After 15 years in program and knowing all that I knew about the disease simply meant I had to get more creative with the BS I used on myself. One of my favorite phrases was: "*I'm redefining my abstinence...*" In retrospect, it wasn't true. I had broken my abstinence (again) and was simply redefining my honesty.

I went through phases of trying to delude myself into believing I was following a program. I had the amazing moving abstinence. What was its definition? Essentially, my abstinence was whatever I was eating on that particular day. I remember at one point the definition of my abstinence was "three meals and a snack," What was my definition of "a snack?" Essentially, anything I ate after dinner... and late into the night. Since I was a "grazer," that "snack" could be more than I ate at the first three meals combined!

It took me a long time to see that if I had an abstinence that Henry VIII could follow comfortably, what the heck did I really have? If abstinence is a lifeboat in the sea of my disease, I was handling it all wrong. I needed to hang on inside the lifeboat and if I got pitched out (had a slip), I needed to declare it as such, climb back in, and learn from my mistakes. What I did instead was drill holes in the bottom of the lifeboat so that the edge of the lifeboat was level with the water line. This way I could say I wasn't being thrown out of the lifeboat, I was just *redefining* the boat. In the long run, what did I have? Nothing. All I had was a way to "save face" at meetings. Sadly, it was more important for me to look good at meetings and look bad outside the meetings than the other way around.

Why did I do this? *Insanity.* Today I look back and realize that *I* didn't do this. I allowed *the disease* to do it to me. Understanding that the little voice that is constantly trying to find the "easier, softer way" *is* my disease was the key to getting on the road to recovery for me.

I also remember going through a phase of eating and then "trying to be gentle with myself." I would come to meetings and say "I ate again last night, but I won't beat myself up over it." The trouble is that I did that over and over. Finally, one day a fellow member asked me: "Isn't eating again last night '*beating yourself up*' too?"

She was right on the money. It's hard to convince yourself through affirmations after the fact when you are deliberately doing things you know are self-destructive. What I couldn't see was that my disease was hard at work, taking perfectly good program ideas and then warping them into why I should be eating! I even remember quoting the Big Book as to why I was eating once during my slips!

Another one I used at one point was: "I can't feel deprived. I can't be on a diet." The question I needed to ask myself was: "Is it _you_ that can't feel deprived or _your disease_ that can't feel deprived?" After all, every one of us is on a "diet." I've been on a no liver diet since I could get out of my mother's house. Anything short of constant bingeing is a diet to my disease. As to feeling deprived? _Please!_

My disease wants to take the balance sheet of recovery and then white out the plusses and put all of the minuses in big bold letters.

You know what my disease _doesn't_ say to me? It doesn't say "You poor thing! You don't get to be out of breath halfway up a flight of stairs! You don't get to wear out your pants in the inseam because the fabric rubs against your enormous thighs! You don't get to live an isolated, dismal life with few friends and even fewer romantic interests."

In some ways, people in program do newcomers a true disservice by trying to play to the diseased portion of their brains. We want newcomers to feel like there is nothing to give up and all to gain. That's just not true. _People in A.A. have to give up drinking_. It's unreasonable to expect that we won't have to sacrifice some things for our recovery. 12 Step programs shouldn't compete with a billion dollar diet industry out there trying to convince people they can have something for nothing. If we are a program of honesty, we shouldn't be playing that same game.

At another point in my slip, my disease convinced me that I should work on the spiritual part of the program. What was that about? Well, trying to focus on the spiritual part means I don't actually have to _do anything_ about stopping the eating! Maybe if I worked on the Steps, the food would magically fall into place! While I truly believe that abstinence is a gift from my Higher Power, I need to meet him (her? it?) halfway and do the footwork.

There is a school of thought in program that says perhaps you should work on the Steps first, and that the food will take care of itself. I have to admit that I have seen the occasional person for whom this was true. The fact is that I think for the vast majority of people, in the "chicken and the egg" discussion, *the food has to be put down first*. Think about this logically: was there ever any discussion in A.A. that people didn't have to stop drinking first? No... of course not. In speaking about those rare cases where they used the Steps first and then got abstinent, I think they are very much the exceptions and not the rule. Sadly, for every one of those rare cases, there are probably a hundred people desperately hoping they can find recovery that way – and to no avail. I often wonder how many people heard of these stories and hung on for years before becoming disillusioned and leaving program convinced it "didn't work."

When people say they are going to "work the Steps" without putting down the food, I have to ask an important question: what about that pesky first Step? It says "we are powerless over food" and yet you're saying "I'll get back to that one." Exactly how is that admitting powerlessness? How do you do Steps 2 through 12 before handling Step 1?

One of the other ways I see the disease work at subverting peoples' recovery comes from trying to find the easier, softer way by setting the bar too low. I have known people who, in addition to being compulsive eaters, have also had bouts of anorexia and bulimia. Having come into the program, they have taken care of one part of their disease, but not the other. I know one person who says her abstinence is "no purging," and that's all – even though she is about 200 pounds overweight. Another person I know claims a 10-plus year abstinence, which she defines as freedom from anorexia – but while also maintaining a much "higher than healthy" body weight. The trouble is even with that low bar, the bulimic still manages to break her "no purging" abstinence on a regular basis. I believe the reason why is that she has yet to stop self-medicating with the food and deal with all aspects of her disease. Putting down one part of our disease without working on the whole problem is another way our disease convinces us we're getting better when we are only achieving limited recovery. In both cases, I believe these people are listening to their disease and trying to avoid the discomfort of a clean abstinence. What they are actually avoiding is true recovery from the disease. I wish it were different – that those half-measure abstinences were of some benefit – but I think in the end, like other half measures, they will avail us nothing.

39

To this day I have to deal with the little voice of my disease that wants to whisper to me about my food. I have to deal with the reality of life and my physiology. I'm not in my 20s anymore and every day I seem to need less and less food to maintain my weight. I want to weigh about 10-15 pounds less than I do, so in the strictest of definitions of the words, I'm *overeating*. If 170 is a healthy weight for you, but you're eating the amount of food it takes to maintain 190... then you are technically *over*eating! So today, I am grappling with eating less than I used to – if I want to maintain a healthy body weight. Meanwhile, that little voice in my head (which I have identified as the disease) is whining: "It's not fair! You've been working so hard on your program!" Out here in California, we have a saying "You want fair – go to Pomona" (the site of our annual state fair).

With the food programs that have concrete, well-defined definitions of abstinence, it's hard to play games if you wander off the trail. However, in the food programs without a pre-defined food plan, it's easy for the disease to try to get you to play games with your definition of abstinence. *My disease loves vagueness.* That's why the last thing it wanted me to do was to get a sponsor. Why? Because then there would be a *third opinion* interpolated in the debate between me and my disease. My disease can beat me hands down, but me and another compulsive eater with my best interests at heart? It's not even a fair fight.

What kind of pain do you want?

Although there is a lot of pain associated with compulsive eating, the pain is subtle, dull, and drawn out. Sometimes when the choice comes up between that dull pain and the sometimes acute pain of emotional distress without the food to numb it, it's easy to make the wrong choice.

I was once at a meeting where a number of people said "I guess I just haven't hit bottom yet." One old-timer later spoke to this and said "Folks... bottom is not the goal here!" She was right. I think for me, there is an almost endless succession of bottoms. They might be interrupted with another foray into getting abstinent, but unless I am willing to do the hard work involved with abstinence, I'm only biding my time until my next relapse – and eventually death.

The fact is that everybody – anybody – can pull the bottom up to wherever they are today. You can get off the elevator wherever you want. As a friend says, "*Surrender is simply joining the winning side.*"

What's the price for this surrender? Sometimes it involves going through emotional pain without the aid of what we used to use to deal with it: food. I have come to understand that sometimes emotional pain is the petri dish for emotional growth. I don't like that because I am an emotional pain-a-phobe.

Food was my pressure valve. When I had an emotional problem, it's what I turned to. While it did provide temporary relief, it didn't provide a solution to the problem. There was no real growth. I was like a rat in a maze that went down the wrong channel in the maze. I would hit my head on the end wall, then back all of the way out of the maze to the beginning – and then go down the same path again! What I needed to do was try an alternate way (not eating), and then – and only then – could I possibly find my way out.

There is a passage in one of the stories in the Big Book that speaks about how we cannot allow our recovery to become contingent on the vagaries of life. We're going to have good days and bad days. We need to divorce our food intake from the "drowning our sorrows" during the bad days and the "celebrations" of the good days. This divorcing of our abstinence from the ups and downs of everyday life needs to happen for long-term abstinence to take root.

I will hear people at meetings saying "just for today I didn't eat." Often, I hear these people saying this time after time. While yes, this is a "one day at a time" program, aren't you truly telling yourself "I won't eat today, but I *might* eat tomorrow." If you do that day after day, a day might come when you give yourself that permission. "A day at a time" is certainly good advice for a newcomer, but if you're much past a few months into your recovery and you're still saying that, you might want to look at the level of your surrender to the recovery process.

I tell my sponsees that there needs to be a commitment to their abstinence. They have to strap in for the amusement park ride they're about to experience and be willing to go wherever that recovery takes them. Sometimes it will be hard, and other times it will be scary, but it will invariably lead upward. And when in doubt, even if you don't believe in a Higher Power yet, why not try asking for help from it?

Living your life in a constant "one day at a time" mode is like walking down a street with 100 bakeries lining one side of the street. The "one day at a time" thinking means you'll stop at each bakery, look in, smell the smells and then say "No! Just for today, I don't eat this," and continue on to the next bakery and do the same thing. The trouble with this mindset is that by the 99th bakery, you say to yourself "You know, I've been _so_ good all this time, I'll treat myself at this one bakery" – and off you go. The key with the "commitment to abstinence" mindset is that you walk down the same street, _but you don't see the bakeries at all_!

There used to be a gruff old-time double winner in my meetings named Frank C. We called him "Cinco de Mayo Frank" because when he mentioned his abstinence date he would say it was on "Cinco de Mayo, 1991." Frank was a biker who looked like a Marine drill sergeant, buzz-cut and all. And just like a Marine drill sergeant, Frank brought his A.A. hardcore attitude to his food program. He used to say, "Whenever I get a new sponsee, the first thing I have them do is get a Big Book. Then, I tell them to write two things on the front page – their name and their abstinence date. After they do that, I say to them in no uncertain terms: 'Okay. _One_ of those two things can change – can you guess which one?'" Frank came from a program that stressed commitment to recovery and expected no less from his sponsees.

In looking back at where I was during my slip, I wanted what the old timers had... but I didn't want to do the work they had been willing to do. I didn't want to work on _recovery_, I just wanted to be _recovered_.

In the "How it Works" chapter of the A.A. Big Book, they speak of three important concepts: _"half measures avail us nothing," "with complete abandon,"_ and _"willing to go to any lengths."_ The problem with half measures is that they often give the _illusion_ that they yield more than _nothing_. What I came to understand through bitter failure and defeat was that even though my half measures looked to be yielding something at the time, eventually it all fell apart and I was indeed left looking back at nothing.

"*We grasp this program as the drowning grasp a life preserver,*" it says in the A.A. readings. The problem is that when it comes to food, the average person is not driven to that level of desperation. As a result, if you want recovery to work, you have to simply imagine you're one of those people who might die soon if they don't get it. After all, if you're trying to work a program based on A.A., shouldn't you be working it like a member of A.A.? Besides, if you don't imagine that you're *one of those people who might die soon*, there might come a day where you actually *do* fit that description. By then it might be too late.

Sometimes the disease also creeps back in slowly. It gets you to start backing off from your program. You need to often reassess and ask yourself, "*am I moving toward or away from my substance?*" Are you coasting? If so, it's important to remember that there's only one way to coast and that's downhill.

Let's not kid ourselves about one more salient point: for many of us, there is an actual physiological withdrawal that happens when we first get abstinent. I had pounded down both sugar and flour to such an extent that on many days it became the main staple of my diet. This is food that gave me a quick hit of both calmness and satiety.

Coming off sugar and flour wasn't easy for me. I spent the first week or two really craving the carbs. I also found that eating non-carb foods meant it took a bit longer for the "full" switch to get flipped. Often in the first few weeks of my non-carb abstinence, I would push away from the table still feeling hungry. If I waited about 20 minutes though, I'd lose that feeling. Eventually, that "lag" went away.

I had to make the decision – not whether or not I'd be uncomfortable – but what type of uncomfortableness I would choose. The difference was that after a few weeks that feeling of uncomfortableness went away. Had I kept eating, that dull pain would have continued.

It comes down to this basic choice of which type of uncomfortableness you want to experience, as well as one other choice:

Who will be making the decisions in your life... you or your disease?

How exactly am I powerless over it?

For 15 years, I would sit in meetings and say "I'm powerless over food." Then I would go out and eat. Then I would come back and say "I'm powerless over food." Then I would eat again. This begs the question: "*Just how powerless did I really think I was?*"

I truly believe that I'm powerless over a bullet in a gun. Do I *really* know that? Well, not totally, but I have never put a gun to my head, and as I'm pulling the trigger say to myself: "*I'll start again on Monday.*" My guess is that there would be no starting over on Monday for me. That bullet in the gun represents true powerlessness. That concept was something that, during my slip, I didn't really believe when it came to the food.

When I went to go eat during those slips, was I saying "the heck with 12 Step programs! I'm done with them and I don't care"? No. I really wasn't saying *anything* to myself, but if I were to stop and consider what was going on in the back of my head, it would have been something like: "I'm going to go break my abstinence, and *when I'm ready I'll come back to program and get my abstinence back.*"

This was the basis for my *illusion* of powerfulness over the food. After all, how many times had I had slips in the past? After every one of them, I had come back and eventually gotten my abstinence back. That was the empirical proof that no matter how much I *said* I was powerless – I really wasn't, was I?

There was the problem. I just didn't understand the concept of powerlessness as it pertained to me and my food. I had seen a perfect example of powerlessness with my alcohol consumption. If I had as little as one drink, it had become physically impossible for me to stay away from the next drink.

With the food, however, I knew that if I "got back into the food," I could work on getting my abstinence back. It might not be easy, I might have to get a new sponsor, might have to go to a lot of meetings for a while, but *eventually* I'd be able to grind that train to a halt – again.

I came to a realization one day after the umpteenth time of diving back into the food. I remember asking myself "Why did I break my abstinence again, after a few months of clean eating?" A little voice in the back of my head said to me "You didn't break your abstinence again, you haven't had any real abstinence since you broke your abstinence years ago."

It was true. I had periods of not eating compulsively, but was that true abstinence? Today, I don't think it was. I was just on another "in" cycle, waiting for the next "out" cycle to begin. I also believe when those types of thoughts – ones that seem downright foreign to me – enter my head (as this one about breaking my abstinence did), it is the voice of a power greater than myself. I'll talk more about this later.

What I truly get in my gut today is a different outlook on the concept of powerlessness when it comes to the food. I understand today that _I_ am power_ful_ over the food – *in the small picture.* What I need to do however, is to pull the camera out for the "wide shot" and look at my whole life in terms of the 12 Step programs for food. For me today, *I get it*: I _am_ power_less_ over the food... _in the big picture_.

When I first came into O.A., people use to practically pound the podium and say "We don't eat, no matter what!" It was a very strident, adamant kind of statement. A while back, I heard the same concept put in a much gentler way. The person said "If you are a compulsive eater, and you've made food an option, it will always be the _only_ option."

This is my great truth about abstinence. The food, if I allow it, will always be the path of least resistance. If I have a choice of going through emotional pain and turmoil, or eating something I enjoy and which – at least at some point in my life – did something to calm that turmoil, it's a no brainer! Of course, I am going to go to the food. That's when I came to realize the _real_ idea of powerlessness. Food _could no longer be an option_ to soothe my emotions. It needed to be fuel for my body – no more, and no less. I could enjoy it, mind you, but I needed to be aware of _why_ I was eating it.

Ironically, once I made that commitment to work _through_ my problems, instead of getting into the food as a way of running away from them, I found life starting to get easier, because I had – finally – taken Step One. I was powerless over the food.

Step 1, Part 2: "And our lives had become unmanageable."

One of the hardest things for many people coming into the various 12 Step food programs is grasping the idea that their lives had become unmanageable. Quite often, they had become super achievers as a way to compensate for their feelings of inadequacy. How then, they would ask, could we say that their lives were unmanageable when they were CEOs, owned businesses, had families, etc.

In most cases, when asked about this, I try to get people to see just how much of their lives are really governed by the food and their character defects – and not themselves. Their disease is or was calling the shots in many aspects of their lives.

I have also heard people in program swap out the pieces of this part of the first Step and say *"I'm powerless over life and my food had become unmanageable."* This is also true.

Some people are ready to change the minute they come through the doors. For others it is when they finally strip away the delusion the disease has tried to foist upon them that "things aren't really that bad." At some point, for recovery to truly start, we must all get to the point of realizing just how badly this disease has affected us. We also have to admit that despite our intelligence and efforts to the contrary, we have been unable to make any significant, long lasting inroads into our disease. It's only when we can admit we need help that things can get better.

We have a three-fold disease: spiritual, emotional and physical. In terms of the spiritual, we are looking for peace, contentment, and to feel good about ourselves. This is the spiritual *dis*ease, which in turn churns our guts up and causes us to have emotional *dis*ease. When we cannot find peace, we turn to the only thing that had ever worked for us: the food. And that is the physical part of the *dis*ease.

Since we got sick in that order, to get well we must work in the reverse order. We work on getting the physical aspect under control so that we can then work on the emotional aspect and then finally the spiritual. That's what the rest of this book is about.

Chapter 4 – Step 2: Back to our Senses

Step 2: "Came to believe that a power greater than ourselves could restore us to sanity."

My Own Best Efforts...

I had an old sponsor who used to say "If you could have stopped by yourself, you'd have done it by now," He was right, but that persistent delusion that around the next corner, that next tidbit of knowledge I gain about my food problem will be the one that allows me to conquer it still persisted. After all, I had conquered so many other things in my life with just my brainpower, why should this problem be so unique?

Yet, as they say in A.A., *"Your own best efforts got you to the point where you were when you dragged your sorry butt through the door."*

It's true. *You can't fix a broken brain with a broken brain.* My disease, which infests every synapse of my brain, will simply take all that I learn about the disease, even within the 12 Step program (*especially* within a 12 Step program) and use that information against me.

So, if the admission of the first Step is that I have a problem and I'm powerless over it, I'm doomed, right?

Not according to the first part of the 2nd Step, which then says: "Came to believe in *a power greater than ourselves*"...

Whoa! A power greater than myself? So you <u>are</u> trying to foist a belief in God on me? This was exactly the kind of thing that made me want to run for the door when I was first presented with the idea of joining a 12 Step program. In fact, this concept, and the "*G Word*" were the major stumbling blocks that I couldn't imagine how to get beyond.

In my story, I spoke about how my first sponsor had helped me see the difference between a spiritual program and a religious program. His assurance that I could be in the program until I was 100 years old, and nobody would ever force me to believe anything, allowed me to quit the debating society. All that was needed for recovery to take root, he promised me, was an open mind on the subject.

For now, however, let's not even talk about God with a capital 'G'. Let's talk about the concept of a *Higher Power*. I'm not even talking about _the_ Higher Power. The key here is not just one Higher Power, but a hierarchy of Higher Power_s_. Before that can happen though, *I need to believe that I am a lesser power.*

Finding the ability to reduce one's ego to accept help and take direction isn't easy – but it is the key to starting to recover in a 12 Step program. When I see someone coming to program saying "I'm not willing to do this or that," I see a person setting themselves up to fail.

However, there is a certain logic in the defiant person's head, based on past experience. They have done well in their lives being the determiner of their actions in many areas, and often they are well above average in intelligence. The idea of saying "Okay, I give up... just tell me what to do" is an anathema to them. That's where the second part of the 2nd Step has to come into play:

"... could restore us to sanity."

Let me let you in on a little secret. 12 Step programs *love* the number twelve. They like it when lists add up to an even dozen – but if you consider them carefully, most of them don't. The Steps and Traditions are not even close. To get to that magic dozen, often two or more thoughts are jammed together into a single Step or Tradition. The 2nd Step is a good example.

The 2nd Step is a two part Step, and in some ways it's backwards, just like Step One. First, there's something we *have to understand*. In Step One, we need to really understand what powerlessness means to us before we can admit we've got a problem. We then have to admit that powerlessness has affected our lives and made them unmanageable (again – two parts). Then we move on to Step Two, where the two parts of the Step are transposed (in my opinion). It's important to first realize we can't trust our own flawed brainpower. That means admitting we're insane – at least in respect to the food. Then – and only then – can we really start seeing ourselves as human and limited – or as that *"lesser power."* Once we can see ourselves as a lesser power, then we can turn to others for help. In other words, Higher Power_s_.

48

This is one of the most maddening things about this disease. We first have to realize we are not sane – at least around the food. This is hard because we're often so sane and intelligent in all other areas of our lives. Addiction however, is a very specific and narrow banded type of insanity. If it were broader – let's say it caused me to start speaking in tongues or all of a sudden I found myself wandering naked down the street – it would be easier to say "Wow... I'm messed up. I better let somebody else tell me what to do." This is another difficult part of the disease... *giving up control.* It's very hard for some of us because at earlier points in our lives, control was essential and not having it was perceived as dangerous. Many of us have carried that overwhelming need for maintaining control into adulthood.

Sponsorship: A bridge between the 2nd and 3rd Steps.

Going back to Step One, the fact there is so much fear and feeling of a lack of control in our lives causes us to develop various character defects to help us feel better. Probably the one of the most basic defects concerns trust – or rather *dis*trust. Getting to the place where we are willing to reach out to another person to say "I need help" is, in many ways, our first act of faith. It might very well be faith borne out of desperation, but any way we reach it, it's an important step.

When we first broach the concept of a Higher Power, the main thing we need to understand is this: <u>*there is a Higher Power, and we're not it*</u>. Most of us didn't have a truly delusional belief that we were God, but we continued to hang on to the faulty belief that we knew what was best for us. What program teaches is that in almost every other area of our lives this might be true, but when it comes to our addiction, very often we're the *last* person we should be listening to for guidance on eating. Why? Mainly because we – or rather the disease that infects our thinking – has a vested interest in getting us the food we want. In contrast, a sponsor has a vested interest in getting us the recovery we need.

Even people of strong faith need to be disabused of the idea that they can – simply with "the counsel of God" – make good decisions about the subject of their addiction. The idea that it's "me and God alone" is grandiose. As it says in the A.A. 12 & 12, "many wise people of faith have counsel." God and I can go somewhere to commune and I can come away being convinced that God told me chocolate was a vegetable. When I run this by my sponsor however, he has a different idea. The problem I have is simple. I don't know what is the voice of my Higher Power and what is the voice of my disease just doing a really good Higher Power impression.

"Only by being willing to take advice and accept direction could we set foot on the road to straight thinking," says the A.A. 12 & 12 (page 59). Yet, I watch so many people ask for help from a sponsor, then immediately either start ignoring their suggestions or lying to them. I always say that lying to a sponsor is "like playing hide and seek with yourself." The bottom line is that if you are lying to your sponsor – you've probably got the wrong sponsor.

The other thing I did for a while was to have a "bullshit sponsor." What is that, you ask? A "bullshit sponsor" is a sponsor you have so that you can tell other people that you *have* a sponsor, but someone you never call or utilize. I had a few of them over the years, and they might as well have been bobble head dolls for all the good they did me.

Picking a sponsor

I've heard people say at meetings "I'm looking for a sponsor that I resonate with." My translation is: "I'm looking for a clone of myself." A passage from O.A.'s "Tools of Recovery" hits the nail right on the head on this subject. "Find a person who has what you want and ask how he or she is achieving it."

When I came to my first food program, I was anti-sponsor. What I really wanted to do was buy every piece of literature, read it, figure out how to "do the program" and then leave. It took me a while to realize that it wasn't a home study course.

Wanting to do it myself made sense in the context of my life, because I was able to do this with so many other areas of my life. God gifted me with a marvelous brain. When I was younger and stupider, I talked my way into a job trouble shooting electronics down to component level. There was only one problem: I had never taken as much as *one* electronics course! I had started to read books on electronics and managed to get the job and ended up as a service department manager! I'm not bragging, just trying to make the point that I can learn almost anything. My brain, however, is of no help to me with my addictive diseases. As the Big Book says *"self-knowledge avails us nothing!"*

I also didn't want a sponsor because I really didn't want to be accountable to another person – especially about my food. I don't want to have to tell someone what I'm eating. I *certainly* don't want to tell someone when I screw up! If you are in a food program with a flexible food plan, I have one critical piece of advice to give: don't work on your food plan alone!

What I tell my sponsees about my job as a sponsor is this: "I will never tell you what to eat, what not to eat, or what to weigh – you get to decide all that. I'm not the food police, but I *am* the honesty police." If a sponsee tells me they are putting bread on his "do not eat" list, and then a few weeks later he tells me he ate bread, I'm going to point out what he must have forgotten, that bread wasn't part of his food plan. I'm the guy who, when the sponsee is disappointed on weigh day about the number on the scale, reminds him about some of the food choices he's made. I also tell him not to feel guilty, but be honest with me about his food. "If you go out and eat," I tell him, "I promise I won't gain a pound... so there won't be any judgment on my part."

Another part of the insanity of the disease is the attempt to find the simple, easy answer. Sometimes there just are no easy answers. A common quest of addicts is looking for that easier, softer way. Early on, I wanted what all of the old timers had, but without doing any of the work they did to achieve it. It took me a long time to realize I wasn't special and I had to trudge the same path everyone else did. The good news was that they weren't special either – that they didn't possess some special abstinence gland that I didn't. If they could do it, I could too.

Having a sponsor that I was willing to talk to about my deepest, darkest secrets was a good thing. As they say in program "stay out of your head, it's a dangerous neighborhood." If I couldn't always stay out of that neighborhood, I could at least let my sponsor know what some of the chatter from "the hood" was saying to me.

I also always say that some of the stupidest things I ever heard were told to me by a sponsor. I would hang up the phone after being given a direction from a sponsor and say out loud "that's the stupidest damned thing I ever heard!". However, I also believed the A.A. concept that says "bitch and moan, but do it anyway," so I would do it. Invariably, whenever I finished doing that "stupid" thing I was told to do, I'd stop and say "that was _exactly_ what I need to do!" Following that "stupid" advice meant I bypassed the defective decision-making committee in my brain. A true definition of being open minded in program is doing what you are sure will fail because your sponsor told you to do it. Being willing to "take direction" is the key to finding recovery. After all, _we don't know what we don't know._

I like my sponsees to commit to attending three meetings a week. That's not to say that there are weeks where they don't, but I ask that they try to make them up at some point. Is there something special about three meetings? Not really, but you have to have a line in the sand somewhere. If you don't have a line, three meetings turns into two, which turns into one every other week... you get the picture. I also like to know my sponsees' food plan, and I like them to weigh themselves monthly.

It's important for me as a sponsor to remember my place. The A.A. Big Book says "_we are not professionals,_" It drives me crazy when I hear stories about sponsors telling sponsees to do things outside their purview, like telling them to stop taking prescribed medications. This is a very dangerous thing, and unless you have an M.D., you have no business doing this.

In the A.A. Big Book, it's not an accident that the 12th Step gets an entire chapter ("Working with Others"). One of the things the Big Book talks about concerns advice giving. We need to watch out about this, especially in domestic matters. It's important to realize that as a sponsor, I'm only getting one side of the story. I also have to remember my limitations. Years ago, I was having some relationship problems with a woman who I was dating. When I went to my then sponsor about it, he said to me "John, I can't help you with this. I'm a gay man and I'm not currently in a relationship." I found that to be incredibly admirable. He had the humility to say "I don't know." It's something I took as a life lesson.

So what are the keys to being a sponsor? Darned if I know. Years ago, I found a book on sponsoring in 12 Step programs. It was a series of questions and answers asked to a group of 12 Step people in various programs. It asked their opinions on a variety of subjects about sponsorship. There were questions like: "If a sponsee is slipping a lot, should you cut them loose or stick with them?" As it turned out the answers were all over the place. Some were absolutely contradictory. With more time in program I realize that this is exactly the way it should be. The reality is that there isn't – and shouldn't be – some cookie cutter formula for sponsoring people who come in all personality types. Some of my sponsees need to have the "beat myself stick" wrested from their hands, while others seem to go out of their way to excuse their actions.

Going to a program for families of addicts and alcoholics made me a better sponsor. It reminded me that I am there to help, not to control. My power as a sponsor is very limited. In my early days in program, I used to have power struggles with sponsees – now I don't. "If you want what I have, try taking my direction," I always tell them. I'm not a control freak, but you have to be willing to try new things. I also have extra parameters for my sponsees. While the 3rd Tradition says "the only requirement is a desire to stop eating," that doesn't mean sponsors can't have more "musts" – and I do.

One of the other areas that sponsorship has helped me work on is my people pleasing. One of the concepts I talk about could be interpreted as controversial (although for me, it is clear). This is my concept of "Mommy love" vs. "Daddy love" and how it pertains to sponsoring. While this idea uses the words "Mommy" and "Daddy," it is totally divorced from the sex of the person involved.

"Mommy love" is that totally unconditional love that always reinforces, no matter what the situation. It is the kind of nurturing that is actually very beneficial to young children. It tells them they are special, and that they can do anything. The shortcoming is that my disease thrives on "Mommy love." It will soak up all that is given and then look for more. An example of it is when a person slips and then hears from a sponsor: "Oh, you poor thing! Don't beat yourself up!"

I used to hear that and think "Okay, I won't beat myself up. In fact, I'll go out again tonight and eat and I won't beat myself up *again*! After all, I have a disease and I'm powerless over eating!" The trouble is that one of the base components of my disease is immaturity, and "Mommy love" feeds that – while providing no real help against the addiction. Yes, the basis of the statement "Don't beat yourself up, it doesn't help" is true on an intellectual level, it can easily be misconstrued by my disease – which wants to keep me in the food.

"Daddy love" (the key here being the word "love") says: "why yes, you *did* screw up. Now how can we learn from it – so it doesn't happen again?" Daddy love requires honesty on my part as a sponsor, which isn't always easy when the person to whom I'm speaking might want that total unconditional reassurance. My job as sponsor, though, is to help him or her beat the disease. It's incredibly important for me to try to "tease" the disease away from the person. I need to be able to focus my sponsoring the way the radiation technician focuses her radiation beam on cancer cells in a human body.

Having grasped the idea that we were not in a right mind about the food and needed some help, we were nearing the point of making the total commitment to jumping in the deep end of the pool.

Chapter 5 – Step 3: Where Reality and Theory Meet

Step 3: "Made a decision to turn our will and our lives over to the care of God as we understood Him."

Perhaps it's time to address the issue that plagues many newcomers: God. I have to admit that even after 30 years in program, I still have trouble with the word "God." There, I said it. I know I'm not the only long-timer who feels that way. Let's first admit that all we are _actually_ talking about here are three letters of the alphabet strung together in a particular order. When I came into program, those letters in that order represented something to me totally different from what I believe today. The word still represented the punitive, judgmental God that was foisted on me by the religion I was born into – which was simply an accident of birth.

Want another three letter word with letters strung in a particular order? Okay, how about "red?" Think about that word for a moment. Conjure up a mental picture of a ball – a _red_ ball. Here's the funny thing... how do you know my "red" and your "red" are the same? Perhaps if you could get inside my brain, you might realize I see red as you see the color blue. It really wouldn't matter, as we've all decided the color on the background of a stop sign is called "red." Its actual color – as registered in our brains – might be different for all of us. We have just made the assumption that red looks the same way for all people. It may not – and in a way it doesn't matter. This is a good analogy for coming to an understanding of God, as spoken of in 12 Step programs.

For me, using the word "God" now means using a "shorthand" for something infinitely complex and individual to each of us. I have stripped away all my pre-conceived notions and made the word a "placeholder." The word has its usefulness, not the least of which is that it's a one syllable word that is universally understood, especially within the rooms of 12 Step programs. I find it easier than the semantically awkward "Higher Power," and it uses 25% of the syllables. Both "God" and "Higher Power" are interchangeable to me, and I use both appellations throughout this book, mainly as a way to not sound too repetitive.

Then there's the nature of what one believes. If you come to program with a pre-defined idea of your Higher Power with which you are comfortable, that's fine. I would contend, however, that you need to find a way to take whatever you believe – or are *going* to believe – and make it something *personal* and useful to *you*. If belief in a God alone were enough to get recovery, I would never have known the Catholic priests and nuns, Protestant ministers and Jewish rabbis and cantors I've met in my 12 Step meetings. What all of those clergy people have told me was that for their recovery to take root, they needed to develop some kind of personal relationship with a Higher Power that they had previously lacked. They especially needed one that they believed would help them with their compulsive eating. I heard one old Irishman say this at an A.A. meeting once: *"I had to hit 60 years of age and join A.A. before I realized I could pray to God without going through Rome."*

I came in my first program as an avowed atheist. I had been raised in a very dogmatic religion (in fact, they invented the word "dogma"), and I had run away from it. I had never had or felt any real connection with a God. Later on in my life, God was Santa Claus. If you wanted me to believe in God, I would posit, then I need you to fulfill this list of things I want – otherwise there is no God. So my first sponsor's daunting task (although he never knew it) was to _prove_ to me that there was indeed a Higher Power, and one that would help me.

A belief in a God is not needed to stay in program and to have recovery through the Steps. One of the things I would suggest _is_ needed is an open mind – especially about the idea of redefining our concept of God or Higher Power. I look back and realize the arrogance of my earlier atheism. Faith is something needed to believe in a God as most societies define it. I would also contend that one also needs faith to say absolutely that there is _no_ God. When prodded on my atheism before I came to program, I would respond angrily "prove there is a God!" While nobody can do this, neither could I prove there is _not_ a God. It might just be that whatever Higher Power there is out there has chosen to not reveal the nature of its presence to us. When asked if there is indeed a God-like Higher Power, I say the same thing: "Darned if I know!" I do believe that for me, _a_ Higher Power – of my understanding – is helping me with my recovery every day.

All of this is a precursor to getting past the words of Step Three: *"Made a decision to turn our will and our lives over to the care of God, as we understood him."*

In terms of the Third Step, if you are still of the totally atheist belief, the word "God" in that Step is going to seem to be a total roadblock. I'm begging you to not allow it to be so. Yes, you will need to find <u>some</u> Higher Power, but it doesn't have to be the guy on the ceiling of the Sistine Chapel. For now, we can make that Higher Power – at the very least – the group of people in your program. Certainly, if they've got any time of putting and keeping the food down and you don't, then they have something to offer that you yourself haven't been able to achieve.

The important thing is that you come to see yourself – at least in terms of the disease – as a *lesser power* in need of help. This understanding, coupled with a desire to get help from another is an invaluable step toward the most important concept in 12 Step programs: *surrender.* The word "surrender" is often seen as a pejorative word. It's fraught with judgment, especially in terms of winning and losing. As the old program expression says, however: *"Surrender is just moving over to the winning side."*

So what exactly does surrender in a 12 Step program look like? In the beginning it can just be getting a sponsor and saying "I don't know what to do, please help me." Surrender then means *taking direction* from that person and diving into the program by working on the Steps and using the Tools. It involves integrating the Steps and the program into your day to day life as much as possible. Sometimes you do the actions without totally believing they're going to work. That's okay – do them anyway. There's a word for that: *faith.*

The idea of "turning over" our will and our lives is another roadblock for many. For a long time when I heard the phrase "turn it over," I responded with "just what the heck does that mean anyway?" I know it meant "turn it over to God," but how exactly one does that I could not fathom. What I have found helpful was to reverse the view of that phrase and see it this way: *I need to simply remove the <u>blockage of self-will</u> in my life.*

Finding a Higher Power of your understanding

One of the earliest things said to me about God was from my first sponsor who said: *"The only thing you have to understand about God is this: you're not it."*

When the meaning of those words hit me, it was very powerful. If there was some guiding force in the world, the only thing I needed to remember was that it wasn't me. There's a sense of relief when you realize you only have to take care of yourself and not the world. I was the "caretaker" personality in my alcoholic family growing up. I had to make sure everyone was happy and everything was running right. I assumed that mantle as an adult and it was exhausting. Now I understood that the world would somehow muddle along without my direction.

I was a major pain to that first sponsor, because I was the "deep thinker" that needed the theological questions of the world to be answered to my satisfaction.

"If there's a God, how can there be things like The Holocaust?" I remember asking. He would get a wry smile and say "Well... if you could understand that, then you'd be God, wouldn't you?" There were definitely days I wanted to haul off and belt my first sponsor. As with almost everything else he told me in those first days, however, he was right.

After I had come to him for about the tenth time with a "if there's a God" question, he stopped me. "Do you think if you were designing a God, you'd have it be different?"

"Yes, absolutely!" I replied.

"Good. Then I want you to write up exactly what you would have God be if you were designing him," he said. Charged with that task, I came back to him in a week or so with my "design document."

I read it to him with great relish. I don't remember exactly what I had written, but something along the lines of "universal love, forgiveness, etc." He looked at me and then poked the piece of paper I was holding and said "Okay... *there's* your God right there." What he had made me do was not unlike what I had heard from other people: make a want ad for my concept of a God. As I have heard said, to find this connection with a Higher Power, often you have to tear down the existing structure to make room for a new *frustrated that people who believe in the idea God ... as their get ... a Christian ... the same I think of Christian should ... who meeting they I am a ... that I don't ... my ... perfect easy*

building. If there isn't a feeling of connection with a God from your past, fire him!

There are as many definitions of God as there are people in program. Many people think of the sea as their Higher Power. It's hard to go to the shore and look out to the horizon at that expanse, then look down at the waves lapping endlessly and not feel a bit smaller. You know you didn't make those waves, nor could you stop them if you wished. There were many things like that in nature. I remember always accepting that there was such a thing as "nature," and that "nature" was responsible for many things in the world that I did not understand. How was it that I could accept "nature" and not "God?" If I'm totally honest about it, it was past prejudices. How about simply thinking of "nature" as one's God, I ask my sponsees now.

For some, they had to banish the Judeo-Christian idea of an external God. Many Eastern beliefs incorporate the idea of a God within us all. The main thing was that I had to find some kind of *personal* connection with that Higher Power that would help me battle my disease. Perhaps you prefer to call it your "better self" rather than an external Higher Power. That's fine as long as it helps you with the food addiction.

This new "design document" was the beginning of a lifelong journey of discovery. One of the most important pieces of writing about this is in "*The Spiritual Experience*," which is one of the appendices of the Big Book. My spiritual experience was like those of so many other seekers: one of the *educational variety*. Slowly over time, I had observed way too many "coincidences" in program to think there wasn't something out there. I believe this is how many program people "come to believe" in something. As many program people ask, "Is it odd, or is it God?"

As the child of alcoholics, trust has always been a problem for me. As a kid, I couldn't trust my parents, the people you were <u>supposed</u> to be able to trust. Take that inability to trust up another level. You want me to be able to trust a *stranger* – no way! These people in the 12 Step program wanted me to not only trust in a stranger, but also something or someone I couldn't even see? You've got to be kidding me!

I also had to unlearn other things from my past, like the idea of a male God. I come from two long lines of nasty Irish drunks.

There wasn't a lot of unconditional love from any of the males from my past. So I had to banish the concept of the male God. Again, I have to look past the "shortcuts" in the Steps and writing where it references "Him," etc. These were written by the early members of the first 12 Step program, which was born from a Christian fellowship.

Allow me a momentary side trip concerning the Big Book. It is a product of its time, and one that could use some updating – mostly in wording, not in content. I need to remember this whenever any of the Big Book or A.A. "12 and 12" readings start to sound a little too "gospel-like." The trouble is that if someone did attempt to update the Big Book, it would immediately cause a schism. There would be "old Big Book" people splitting off from "new Big Book" people. There are already paroxysms of anguish when a new edition comes out with new stories in the back of the book. People like the Big Book the way it was when they came in. *But I digress.*

When I was new to the 12 Step rooms, it was deathly important to me that I figure out <u>exactly</u> what my belief was concerning a Higher Power. I find today (and I hear this from a lot of long-timers) that I don't spend a lot of mental energy on it any more. An old adage says: "God can't be understood with the head, it can only be felt with the heart." In the end, the words from that first sponsor sums it all up: *"The only thing you have to understand about God is this: you're not it."* If you'll excuse the joke: Amen!

The A.A. Big Book's thesis sentence has been said to be: "*Its [the Big Book's] main object is to enable you to find a Power greater than yourself which will solve your problem*" (p. 45: "We Agnostics"). I think its purpose is actually to get the addict to see himself as a lesser power so as to become teachable and be open to new ideas.

Is there a God? I don't know for sure. My belief today is more of the thought that "everything is happening exactly the way it is supposed to be." I don't believe in a guy with white robes and a beard. I don't really even believe in an afterlife. If there is one, great. If not, I guess I won't really be aware – just like I wasn't aware of anything before I was born. I'm pretty accepting of death. Even if I wasn't accepting of this inevitability – what can I do about it? Nothing. My Higher Power is more like "the force," and my belief is that everything is as it should be. My job is just to accept it. If I am wrong about this philosophy, what's the worst thing that's happened? I led a more peaceful life.

I know that today I am no longer the fearful person I once was. I didn't walk around with a lot of fear on the surface, but I was an angry person, and in examining that anger, I found lots of fear underneath it. On any given day, there are loads of things about which to be fearful. Don't believe me? Go pick up a newspaper. Watch the all-news TV channels. Yikes!

Here's an example of why finding a faith is important. I have been self-employed since the early 1980s. When I tell people that, I often hear "Oh, I could never do that. I need the security of a job with a big company."

I can understand that. So let's say you went to work for a large company – even the third largest company in the United States. The job was in a huge skyscraper in the middle of a major city – let's call it Houston – and that company employed many thousands of people. Now let's give that company a name: *Enron.* On a particular day a few years ago, thousands of people who felt that they had a secure job with a large corporation turned up for work at that big skyscraper in Houston, only to find the doors locked and the company gone. How's that for scary?

A line from a famous play I love said "Reality is a collective hunch." I think the same can be said about security. I need faith in something other than myself otherwise this is a really scary world. As has been said, faith and fear cannot co-exist for long. The security we so strive for is almost always the *illusion of security* – like what those Enron employees had. *men*

My favorite story about faith came from a conversation I had with my mother one day. I kept trying to get her to come out to the West Coast for a visit, but she was deathly afraid of flying. Meanwhile, she had re-immersed herself in the religion of her birth. I asked her, "If you believe in God and have faith, why are you so afraid of flying?"

She answered my question with another question: "So you think that God will protect you from a plane crash every time you fly?"

I laughed. I said "Mom, I live about 500 feet away from a runway at Santa Monica Airport. If God wants me to die in a plane crash, I can be sleeping in my bed and he'll bring the plane to _me_!" I never did get her to fly west to visit me.

The thing I really love about the 12 Step view of spirituality and God is that it really isn't some woo-woo vision of spirituality. It is a spiritual view that is integrated with real life. It says that it's good to have prayer and meditation with a Higher Power, but that we should also be calling our sponsors and doing the deeds and service that need to be done day-to-day. We can call on our Higher Power for help all of the time, but we still need to be the ones doing the footwork. It says that despite all of our lofty ideals, we're still human and we're going to fall on our face from time to time and that it's okay. We pick ourselves up and try to do better next time.

Even if you have a rock steady belief in God, there's something we can agree on: chances are that God was around before 1935, but people were dying of alcoholism with no hope of recovery. Priests, ministers, and rabbis were of little help. The same could be said about compulsive eating. Before 1960, if you were a compulsive eater, you were probably doomed to that pitiful and incomprehensible demoralization we all felt. There was a good chance you would have a shortened or at least diminished life.

Today, one of the items on my gratitude list is that I was born in a time where I had a _chance_ to find recovery. As I heard someone say once: "The 12 Steps were God's gift to the 20th Century."

The gifts of finding a Higher Power

To me, the biggest gift of finding a Higher Power _of my understanding_ was finding a new perspective for looking at life. I was able to lose some of the self-centeredness that had been amplifying all of my problems for years. When you live in a prison of self as I did, everything that happens is a personal attack or affront, and thus intensified. I also felt a real need to assign blame to everything that happened. Now, I can see life as the old (cleaned up) phrase goes: _"Stuff happens."_

That "need to blame" was a killer. It stood like a huge roadblock between me and my problems on any given day. Very often, I had to stew in the "why" for quite a while before I rolled up my sleeves and worked on whatever problem had provoked the "why." Here is a truism I have come to see:

62

"Why?" is the most useless word in the universe. If you're asking "Why?" it's undoubtedly because something happened in a way that you *didn't* like (when was the last time you said "*Why!?!?! Why did I hit the lottery?*"). So if you do get your "why" question answered exactly the way you want (which is about 0.1% of the time), *you're exactly where you started*. If, on the other hand, you don't get the "why" answered the way you want it, you're frustrated and feel life is unfair. Solution: lose the word "why" from your daily vocabulary. It will allow you to simply address the situation at hand and find a solution – and you'll be a lot happier.

Getting out of the prison of self also meant I became a lot less paranoid about things. When everybody's actions are tied via an invisible string back to you, everything is personal. That guy who cut me off on the highway? He did it to me deliberately – and I must exact revenge!

No... the reality of life is that a lot of times people are just clueless. The guy who cut me off was probably talking on the phone, perhaps was in an argument with his wife and *had no idea* that he was cutting me off! One of my favorite quotes goes something like: "What would really bother me most about what people think about me is just *how little* time they actually spend thinking about me."

The other great gift in life is the removal of fear. I used to spend a huge amount of my time in projection and fear. Coming from my alcoholic childhood, it was imperative that I was ready for whatever came at me. As a result, I spent a lot of time thinking about what possible problems were ahead for me right over the horizon. Worrying about life was a chess game to me, and I always had to run it out fifteen moves in advance.

I had somehow mistaken worrying about a problem as being *the same as doing something about it.*

If I ran any possible problem out to the worst case scenario, somehow I could get ahead of it, I had surmised. No, it only traumatized me. This was because *my* worst case scenario was absurdly past what the *real* worst case scenario was. I also somehow devised an arbitrary upper limit on my worrying. The *real* worst case scenario is a meteor hits Earth which destroys all life or I'm going to drop dead. Somehow I had decided *those* possibilities were absurd.

In reality, there is some comfort to be found in feeling that having more information can help with a problem. It is why so many people were glued to the television in the days after 9/11. We somehow felt if we _knew more_, the world would be less scary. The reality is that the things I worry about almost _never_ happen and the things that _do_ come, I couldn't see coming. Nevertheless, I handle these problems – foreseen or not foreseen – just fine. Or I should say _we_ handle them fine – myself and my Higher Power. The more I can believe this on a gut level, the less time I spend obsessing on problems that are not yet upon me.

I heard one old timer say at an A.A. meeting once: "Projection _always_ works. I know this because everything I worry about _never_ happens!"

What all of those exhausting mental gymnastics were really about was fear of things outside my of control. What I was grasping for, of course, was merely more of that _illusion_ of control. In the end, whenever I spend any time drilling down into the realities of life's problems, I find I have finite control over almost everything.

When we get down to it, the whole 12 Step process easily reduces (to use a cooking term) to three simple lines:

"God, grant me the serenity to accept the things
I cannot change,
Courage to change the things I can,
And the wisdom to know the difference."

When talking about the Serenity Prayer, I used to have a sponsor who would pinch the skin on the back of his hand and say "See this? Here's your 'difference' right here. Everything from the skin inwards... things you can change. Everything outside the skin... things you cannot change." Truer words were never spoken.

What are our main fears? The Big Book states it simply: _"Fear of not getting what we want, and losing what we have."_

One of the other problems I have with my fears is my own grandiosity. I am self-employed and my work flow goes through good times and bad times. When I hit a bad time, does my mind say "Well, here's another one of those bad times you've weathered a dozen times before?" Nope. My catastrophizing brain has me living under a bridge in a box and selling oranges at the end of the highway off ramp. The personality difference between the old me and the new me is that when those thoughts pop into my brain I can laugh and know it's just my grandiose brain at work again. The fact is that if there was an economic depression tomorrow I would be okay. I have a great brain, good work ethic, and I'm also very creative. Either I would find a way to make money as an entrepreneur, or I'd go to work for somebody. I believe I could always find work as I'm exactly the kind of employee people want. Would I make as much as I would like to? Probably not. Would I be doing something "fulfilling"? Again, I'm guessing not. Yet, I would not starve and I'd muddle through. More importantly, I would have a gut level belief – call it a belief in a Higher Power or whatever you like – that everything would turn out all right.

The longer you stay around 12 Step programs, the easier life gets – especially when rough times hit. This is because rough situations were the first place we learned to step back and try to consider how the concept of a Higher Power might fit into the mix. The more we did this, and practiced this, the better we got at it. I can understand religions that want their members to stop and pray at certain times of the day. It's probably not the time that is important, nor what the prayers say – but rather that the members stop at regular intervals and think about themselves in the bigger picture of the world and their place in it. Taking time during the day to get some perspective about life has its advantages.

When people ask me about my concept of a Higher Power I tell them, "It's simple... I keep my Higher Power in my wallet." By that I mean that I have two paragraphs from the Big Book in my wallet: the "Acceptance paragraph" and the one immediately following it (page 417). Grasping the concept of acceptance was truly life changing for me. The first thing I had to understand was that accepting something didn't mean I had to _like_ it – just accept it.

The majority of my problems were proportionally amplified by the distance between reality and the way I thought things _should be_. This is especially true about any change, which my inner five year old _hates_. One of my favorite lines is: *"Change isn't painful... resistance to change is painful."*

And for us, the next change would be throwing ourselves headlong into recovery.

Chapter 6 – The Decision Made, We Need Tools

To review the Step process so far, in Step 1, we began to understand we had a problem. In Step 2, we came to believe that there was something or somebody who seemed to be able to help (or people at least able to help themselves where we could not). In Step 3, with or without the help of a formalized God, we've made a decision to turn our will and our lives over to the care of _something_ now – or at the very least _get out of the way_. If you've made it this far, you've made a commitment to abstinence and the program.

I have a theory about the disease and how the program, the Steps, and the Tools of Recovery work together to help us conquer the demons in our lives. I believe that the first three Steps are the "give up" steps. It's the place we've gotten to so that we can really begin to arrest the physical aspect of the disease – eating compulsively – a day at a time. Moving forward, for the true long-lasting recovery to happen, we have to stay stopped and move to put food in its proper place so that we can work on the rest of the Steps.

Getting the food to "stay stopped" and getting some time with abstinence is what the first three Steps help achieve. To help achieve this state, I believe the Tools of Recovery used in O.A. (and other food programs) are needed. The Tools help us to work the "nuts and bolts" of abstinence on a daily basis. Getting a decent amount of time under your belt with regard to the food is important. Having a year of abstinence is different from having a year of abstinence with "brief vacations" of bingeing in the middle. It's not unlike the difference between a runner that runs a 26.2 mile marathon and a runner that runs for a mile then sits down, then runs again for a mile – and does this for 26.2 miles.

The disease, however, is broken up (at least for me) into the primary disease and the secondary disease. The primary disease is the day in, day out battle of sticking to a food plan, not overeating, calling your sponsor – and working the Tools in general. It's the secondary disease that usually brings down those with long-term abstinence. For true long-term recovery, one has to do the _real_ work involved with the Steps. Invariably, when I see people with more than a year of recovery "go out," it is because they stalled in working all of the Steps and integrating them in their lives.

As I said earlier, getting abstinent and working the Tools is the equivalent of bolting the front and back doors of a house. This is good to prevent a primary assault from an intruder (like our disease), but if we have not worked on the Steps, then we've left the side windows wide open!

My first time around in program, my friends and I were young and thought we were hip, slick and cool. We went to meetings, got together for fellowship, gossiped on the phone to each other and had a great time. We would joke about all those old fogeys that were constantly talking about the Big Book and the Steps. If we had to hear them jabber on about the Steps at one more meeting, we were going to scream!

Then I had my relapse and went to another program for a number of years. When I came back around the original program again, all of those cool friends were gone. You know who was still around? All those old fogeys with the Big Book in one hand and the Steps in the other. As I heard someone say a while back, "My first time around the program, I worked the Tools. This time around I work the Steps."

This is an important distinction. As I have heard said, "it's called a 12 _Step_ program, not a 12 Tool program, or a 12 meeting program." The first time around, I wasn't working the program, I was just doing that aforementioned _"dieting with group support."_

Food Plan and Goal Weight

A note to those who are in a food program with a specific food plan:

This next section, as it pertains to food plans, is probably not needed for you. It's mainly geared for people in food programs without a specific food plan. For those in other programs, the advice is simple: follow your program's food plan and don't get creative with it – otherwise you're missing the whole point.

Now we need to roll up our sleeves and get to work. We need to first look at where we are weight-wise, and then decide where we want to be. If we don't do those things, how can we adequately design a food plan to help us meet our goals? Recovery from this disease might be something of a "chicken and egg" conundrum, but as has been said many times in 12 Step rooms: "we can't think our way into right acting, we need to act our way into right thinking." Translation: quit trying to kick the can down the road about your food – that's your disease talking. You may have heard the program axiom "Working the food without the Steps is a diet." This is absolutely true. Here's another one: "Working the Steps without putting down the food is... Al Anon." (Al Anon is a perfectly good program to help you integrate the 12 Steps into your life, but one that will do nothing to help you with your food addiction.)

A note to those who don't have weight to lose:

For some people coming into the program, weight loss is not an issue. Some people are anorexic, or bulimic, or just driven into program by the constant obsession with the food. For those people I would say, working out a food plan is *still* the touchstone of recovery. A well thought out food plan will give you the freedom to go live your life fully and not obsess on the food 24 hours a day. Yes, some of what follows about weight and scales might not apply to you, but the concept of food being out of proportion in your life probably does apply – and therefore figuring out how to handle it will be important. *Any* kind of unhealthy behavior around food needs to be addressed.

In the many years of working with sponsors, I have tried being flexible about how to design a food plan with sponsees that will best attack their problem. There are those who say "start with a loose abstinence, and then tighten up as you continue." I wish I could say that I found that works, but invariably it does not. Sponsees who have insisted on doing it this way never last for me. I think it is because the disease still had a grip on them and was dictating what food they would or would not give up. They are still negotiating with the disease. I have found that I cannot have a negotiation with my disease – it always gets its way. The willingness to go to any lengths with those in "negotiation mode" just wasn't there. If I have one piece of advice, it is "start with a tight abstinence, and then loosen up later." A very common phrase heard when I first started in program was "when in doubt, leave it out."

Another idea I adopted from an old sponsor was that if we changed my food plan, it could not be changed again for at least 30 days. I think this is a good rule of thumb to prevent "the amazing moving abstinence" – the convenient redefining on the fly if various urges hit. Chances are that if you are considering doing this, you might have a problem with something *other* than food that needs to be addressed.

Deciding on a goal weight is a tricky thing. We can get crazy about it and aim for an unattainable goal, or we can be way too easy on ourselves and set an inordinately high goal weight. When in doubt, look at the various government charts and then add 10 pounds. I think if you have been overweight by a decent amount, it's going to be very hard to hit those government guidelines. Secondly, if you're like me and not in your 30s any more (to put it mildly), that government chart goal becomes doubly hard to hit. Besides, if you do find yourself getting to that slightly higher number with ease, you and your sponsor can always reassess the situation.

In O.A., the new definition of abstinence includes the phrase "while maintaining or moving towards a <u>healthy</u> body weight." Healthy is the key word. It's not about thin or fat, attractive or unattractive – it's about being *healthy.* For me, it's also about being the kind of human being my Higher Power intended. When I was a kid, one of the nasty names they used on me was "elephant." Here's the thing: an elephant is the perfect weight for an elephant. It is built to be that weight, with its legs working like lodge poles to hold itself up. It doesn't have the same kind of design we humans have.

Humans aren't designed to be 300 pounds or more. Ironically weight, *in any form,* is the something to watch. When I was younger, there was a diet doctor named Irwin Stillman who used to say "your heart and body don't know the difference between 50 pounds of fat and 50 pounds of muscle. They just know that they have 50 more pounds to drag around." This is not 100% correct, but I understand what he was trying to say.

As I told one morbidly obese sponsee of mine: "Your car isn't designed to travel at highway speeds in first gear. Yes, you can drive it at highway speeds in first gear. It won't like it, it will whine like crazy, but it will do it. It just won't do it for long before it breaks down, because it wasn't designed to run at those RPMs." The same is true with the human body. I could get away with being 100 pounds overweight in my 20s. I had a sturdy constitution and when you're in your 20s you're practically indestructible. Go to a high traffic place like a mall and look around for the 300-400 pound person over 50. Do you see many? Chances are you won't. So you have to ask yourself where are they? Chances are they are dead – or housebound due to infirmity. That's the reality and future we are facing.

I have a pet peeve in the 12 Step rooms for food, and that is when we applaud peoples' weight loss. It reminds me of Weight Watchers. I'm sorry, but I'm not impressed with someone who has lost 100 pounds. Know why? Because I did it on more than one occasion! Now talk to me about *keeping it off* for 5, 10, and 20 years – that's when you get my applause. That's the real goal we have to be striving for – *long-term* abstinence and weight loss. Whenever I see commercials for some new weight loss drug or regimen, I think about how many of those I've seen in the past. It's like the commercials for gym equipment. If any of them were any good, there wouldn't need to be new ones coming out every month, right? Also I would love to interview some of these "success stories" a year or two later – when the cameras are no longer on them. More than one well-known "winner" of a reality series about weight loss has gained all of his or her weight back – and more.

Another strange aspect of 12 Step programs concerns the person who comes in having to lose 200 pounds and loses 100 of it. Then they plateau out at a weight significantly above a healthy body weight. Still, they get up at meetings and talk about their weight loss, and people applaud. Take a person coming in to program with that same 100 pounds to lose. If they didn't lose anything, would people applaud that? It's a strange phenomenon. To me, this is one of those people who came in and chose an "easy abstinence." In the beginning it's going to work because when you're 200 pounds overweight - just not bingeing every day will accomplish weight loss. This is why I recommend not choosing an easy food plan in the beginning, as it's your time of greatest surrender. As soon as you get comfortable, there's no way to know if your disease will wrest the control away from you and tell you everything is okay, even though you're 100 pounds overweight.

Plan of Eating

My disease loves vagueness about the food. The trouble is that if I don't have a line, how will I ever know if I went over the line? In baseball, there's this thing called a "warning track" – a patch of dirt before the outfield wall. Before this was invented, baseball players chasing fly balls would be so intent on catching the ball that they would run headlong into the wall and not realize it until they regained consciousness. The warning track lets them know they're about to hit the wall. I think this is an important component of all food plans and abstinences – knowing when you're heading toward problem eating.

Designing a good plan is not as easy as it sounds. My abstinence needs to be strong – but not *brittle*. I saw this with that other program phenomenon when I was in another program with very stringent parameters on food. People would toe the line for a while, but then when they weren't perfect, they would go "off the wagon" with abandon and disappear for months at a time before reappearing heavier – often a *lot* heavier.

Maintaining an abstinent food plan can be likened to standing astride a steeply pitched roof. When you're in that kind of situation, you can roll off in either direction. The one direction you can roll off in is having too _loose_ a food plan so that you say "Oh well, I ate a lot, but it's not a break of abstinence and I won't beat myself up about it!" The trouble is that it's very easy to then find yourself excusing that kind of eating a couple of times a week. If you're the kind of addict that I am, those incidents will become increasingly frequent. The other side of that steeply pitched roof is just as deadly. That way says "I ate an extra _pea_ I shouldn't have, so now I'm not perfect. What the heck, now that I'm not perfect, I might as well go out and enjoy myself."

Later on in this book, I will talk more about character defects, especially how they work against us with respect to getting and staying abstinent. One of the worst ones, in my opinion, is perfectionism. As I have heard people say, "The 'ism' in perfectionism stands for 'I sabotage myself'." Someone I respect says *"perfectionism is the conjoined twin of compulsive eating."*

Before I work on a food plan with a sponsee, I often like to ask them to write out a food history. This is a history of their eating and the various attempts at getting to a normal weight over the years. I also ask them to be specific on things like particular binge foods. I ask them to talk about foods that used to be a problem in the past and foods that are a problem now. Sometimes, those two things are not the same. I used to have a terrible problem with candy and ice cream when I was younger. My main *bête noir,* when it comes to food these days are not those foods, but various bread products.

One of the best ways I've heard for compulsive eaters to categorize foods is by using the "red light, yellow light, green light" method. Red light foods are the foods I can never trust myself to eat "like a gentleman." Green light foods are food I eat, but with which I have no trouble eating in proper amounts. Yellow light foods are those that fall in between the two. I often joke that I know my red and green light foods but that 90% of my yellow light foods are foods that *should* be red light foods, but instead (to use the traffic light analogy) I'm hitting the accelerator and trying to run the light.

How do you decide which category is right for the various foods? I think the green light foods are simple, and ironically an awful lot of them are actually colored green (vegetables). There are the foods you know you can't have a normal relationship with – and those are the *severely* red light foods. Then comes the hard part: parsing the remaining foods and trying to be honest as to which really belong in the "red light" pile. Again, I would recommend the old "when in doubt, leave it out" – especially in the beginning. The hardest part in this process will be ignoring your disease, which will be screaming in your ear to *"leave them in!"* A good compromise might be to tell yourself that you can, at some later date, revisit those problematic foods. In other words, make yourself a "just for today these foods are red" bin. That later reassessment, I would add, should be done with the assistance of a sponsor.

Here's an example of the categories I like to mention: I like broccoli, and actually like it a *lot*. It's probably my favorite green vegetable. The thing that makes it different from a red light food is that I don't eat it at a meal and *while* I'm eating it, I'm starting to think about when I'm going to be able to have it again. Foods that have that effect on me need to be in my "red" section.

Another thing I have to do from time to time is to revisit this list. I was in program and abstaining for over a decade when I decided to revisit my dysfunctional relationship with bread. I finally decided that if I wanted to lose some weight, I could no longer "dance with the devil" concerning bread. Over the years, I had stopped eating bread, and then taken it back time and time again. One of the signs that there's a food you can't handle is if you tell yourself you will only have it once in a great while, and then slowly the definition of "great while" becomes shorter. That's what happened to me with bread.

Having had the bread "taken away" from me (with my fingernails still firmly dug into it), after a few days I saw a remarkable thing: I was no longer hungry between meals. This is one of the signs for me about "trouble foods." I need to stay away from foods that mess with my blood sugar levels. Being a recovering alcoholic, I believe I am particularly sensitive to this. I heard a talk on the web a while back from a person who was both a dietician and a recovering alcoholic. She insisted that all recovering alcoholics should severely limit their carb intake. Whether this is a hard and fast rule for all alcoholics, I do not know. I do think for _this_ alcoholic it is definitely the case.

When I was in another food program with a strict food plan, while it was easier at first, I began to see the flaws in that system. Seeing a program that required its members to follow a strict food plan played into my desire to make food and alcohol addiction the same thing. If I could do this, things would become a lot simpler. Being able to apply the black and white of drinking or not drinking to my food problem was a very enticing prospect.

All of my wanting to equate those two substances, however, just didn't make it so. Still, that other stricter program promised me weight loss in return for the strict adherence to that food plan, and at that time it was all I wanted. As promised, by following that food plan to the letter, I lost all the weight. Then I was at my goal weight and I'm still eating _their_ food plan. Eventually, I began to rebel against the food plan, which I saw as an authority figure. Around me in that program, many people were doing the same thing. They would be on these cycles of coming in, losing weight, rebelling, and going out – over and over again. Meanwhile, very few of them were moving on in the Steps in a way outlined in the Big Book. It was, as I said before, "_dieting with group support._"

When I ended up back in a food program where you define your own food plan, I began to understand the difference between the two programs. That other restrictive program was like high school, while the one I moved into was like college. Think about the analogy: in high school, if you didn't go to class, somebody got a phone call. In college, if you don't go to class, the administration feels "Hey, you're paying how much a credit and not going to class? Fine! You're an adult and as such we assume you can make adult choices."

Over the hill (as we say in L.A.), in the San Fernando Valley, is a wise old program veteran. My favorite line from him is: "Today, I eat _what_ I want, _when_ I want it, and _as much_ as I want... _if I'm willing to pay the price_. And today I am _not_ willing to pay that price, so I eat three weighed and measured meals with nothing in between." Here's the funny part: what he describes as his food plan is exactly the food plan from that program I had earlier rebelled against. The difference is that I was using that _program's_ food plan, whereas this long-timer is using _his_ food plan. He has taken ownership of it and as a result, there is nobody against whom to rebel!

Before I went over to the program with the strict food plan, I was convinced I had hit the age where I could no longer lose weight. A funny thing happened when I started following a highly defined food plan: I lost about 15 pounds the first month. So much for my "_slow metabolism._" The fact is that I _do_ have a slow metabolism, but that means that I have to be even more ready to look at all aspects of my food intake. At my age, weight gain comes from the "death by a 1,000 cuts" scenario. There isn't a binge to blame it on, just a little bit more here and more there, etc. As I said earlier: "The price of abstinence is eternal vigilance."

By the way, in the interests of full disclosure, here's what is involved with my food plan: the three things on my "do not eat" list are bread products (unless I'm having a sandwich), melted cheese and butter and deep fried chips. I also try to avoid sugar and other high carb products, but I'm a bit less restrictive about those. I tend to stick to three meals a day, with an evening snack, which is essentially a deferred dessert. My breakfast is always one of two things, a specific brand of cereal and some fruit or some form of eggs and meat (sometimes with a potato product). The latter tends to be a "special" breakfast – often on weekends. Lunch is also usually one of a few things. This might seem dull to some people, but I find it works best for me to keep my meals from getting too "sexy." As I heard someone say once: *"Take the creativity out of your food and put it in your life where it belongs."* Dinner is the one place where I tend to be more creative and is the one place I need to be vigilant.

There are a number of funny things I realized about my eating along the way. I used to tell myself that I loved a good baked potato. Then I went to the other program where a baked potato was "allowed," but with only <u>one</u> pat of butter. What I realized after I ate the yellow part of the potato was that I didn't want any more of the potato. To me, the baked potato had always been a "butter delivery system," and that the reason I liked it was that I would end up eating a half a stick of butter with it. Since eating a half a stick of butter alone was obviously considered gauche, I needed the potato to deliver that butter to me in a socially acceptable manner. Another big binge food of mine when I was younger was potato chips. Then someone years ago (before the major brands started making them) came out with baked, salt-free potato chips. That's when I realized I really *didn't* like potato chips, I liked grease and salt and the potato was just a "delivery system" for that grease and salt. Again, it's all about getting honest with yourself and your foods.

Once I work out a food plan with a sponsee, it's up to the individual sponsee if he wants to "call in" his food every day. By "call in" I mean they write down what they're going to eat and tell me. Some will then bookend it by telling me the next day if they had to deviate from the previously committed food. Some of my sponsees do this, and some of them don't. One of the things I do ask of them is to weigh in once and month and report on the weight change. There are some basic things about physiology and weight that can make regular weighing another good "denial buster." If a person is 300 pounds, and devises a food plan that he thinks will bring him to a goal weight of 180, I'll give him some guidance. At the end of the day, it's his choice as to what he decides. If, however, as a result of that food plan he comes and tells me he's only losing one pound a month, then it is my job to explain to him that he's probably *never* going to reach that goal weight. The fact is that if a 300 pound person is only losing a pound or two a month, he's eating a lot more than he needs to – if he wants to get to 180. If he tells me he's following exactly a food plan that gives him four ounces of protein at a meal, and he's only losing a pound a month... well, we've got to have a talk about the program of honesty.

There is a certain "slope" to weight loss and obviously that loss will be a lot more per month when you are heavier. It then tends to start to "level off" as we get to a lower weight. If, however, that "leveling off" starts at too high a number, I recommend that they think about cutting their intake, or look at the food choices they are making. Some of these concepts are truly not rocket science. If you want to weigh 180 pounds, you just have to eat the amount of food that a 180 pounder eats. It also doesn't hurt to change your lifestyle and exercise regimen as well, but we will talk about that later.

Let me take a moment to talk about scales. As I said, I call them my "denial busters." A food scale and a weight scale help me keep the disease from warping my reality.

It was very important for me — especially when I was new in program – to weigh and measure my food. I have a disease that will allow me to see a huge T-bone steak and say "Yeah... that looks like four ounces!" Sometimes having a scale helps me in the other direction and I find I have been *under*estimating my food intake. I don't take scales to restaurants – although I understand people who do. After a number of years I have gotten to know what four ounces of protein looks like (what I need per meal). It's also just another level of surrender that "keeps the door locked" against my disease. I saw a BBC television special about weight. In England, they did a study of people working to lose weight. These people were writing down their food, but were also being monitored. In every case, these people – honest people knowing they were being monitored – were underreporting their food by about 30%. This is why, at least in the beginning months, it's important to have some "checks and balances" about your food.

Then there is the body weight scale. I hear people in program sometimes say "I used to be a slave to the scale, now I *never* weigh myself!" Well, I used to be a slave to the *food*, does that mean I should I never eat again? I think we need to find moderation in all things and weighing on the scale is a perfect example. I tell sponsees in the weight losing times to weigh only once a month. When I used to sponsor females (I no longer do), I would tell them to weigh not on a calendar month, but at the same point in their menstrual cycle (if they are still in that age range). I think it's important to use the same scale, as it's about gauging the change more than the actual number.

The other thing about weight loss that I have found is that it is just not linear. As you graph your weight loss, it won't be a nice straight line. I have found that it tends to be more of a "stair step" situation. I think this is because your body compensates as you restrict your food – trying to go into conservation mode. After a while, it lets go of more weight, then again goes into conservation mode – and so on. By all means, don't let the number rule your life and moods. We are in this for the long haul, so in a month where you don't have the progress you think you should have – it shouldn't bother you. If you keep doing the things you know you should, you will get to where you want to go. A wise friend once told a sponsee: "*You worry about the fork, let God worry about the scale.*" Being the smart aleck I am, I once told a sponsee who was all atwitter about his lack of weight loss one month: "if a number on a scale is really important to you, cut off a leg – that should give you a number you like." (It's not easy having an ex-comedian as a sponsor some times.)

I also had to look at the fact that my metabolism was slowing down as I got older – which meant less food. There was a part of me practically screaming "That's not fair! I've been working my program, going to meetings... I shouldn't have to cut my food *again*!" The fact is that I didn't *have* to... *if* I was willing to pay the price. The price in this case was a higher weight. Once I removed the disease of compulsive eating from the equation, I was left with the same decision everyone on Earth has: "how much do you want to eat?" vs. "how much do you want to weigh?" For me, it meant I had to increase my exercise and reduce my food – a simple solution, just not easy. As I have heard said, *"you can do what you want, or you can get what you want."*

One of the other things needed for me was more forethought when it came to planning my meals. It was easy when I could just graze my way through the day, but once I made a commitment to my food plan, I needed to be constantly thinking ahead. Sometimes I needed to be inquisitive, as when I had to go to a meeting of a professional group. The easiest default food for many groups is pizza, which I don't eat. I try to be flexible, but I just don't eat certain things and I won't allow peer pressure to cause me to break my abstinence. Even though it's a well-worn phrase, nothing can be truer than *"failing to plan is planning to fail."* And despite my disease screaming "you've *got* to eat" in my head, it just wasn't true. Even in social situations, if you tell people you're a little under the weather, they'll usually leave you alone if you choose not to eat. Then you can enjoy the interactions, instead of obsessing on the food. You can always eat later.

Action Plan

One of the newest Tools in O.A., as of this writing, is the "Action Plan." For many people, this is a point of confusion, and like many things in program, it can consist of many different things, depending on a person's needs. As an old sponsor liked to remind me, "action" is the key word in our program. "That chapter in the Big Book is called 'Into Action,' not 'Into Thinking'," he would say, adding "and thinking is _not_ one of the tools."

For some of us, it wasn't simply a matter of eliminating certain foods, we also had to limit certain food *behaviors* as well. A number of people I know include not eating in the car as part of their abstinence. Others believe in mindful eating – meaning when they eat, it's the only thing they do – they don't turn on the TV when eating, they don't read or do anything that distracts from the experience of eating and enjoying their meals.

Another thing I always ask my sponsees to do is to have an "emergency preparedness plan" figured out. Out here in L.A., with earthquakes a constant threat, it's suggested that you have such a plan in case an earthquake hits in the middle of the night. The same should be true for people trying to battle the disease of compulsive eating. You never know when the overwhelming urge to eat is going to hit, and it can happen at any time. For a lot of us, that urge mostly rears its ugly head in the middle of the night.

There's the old A.A. plan – which goes back to the beginning – of having a collection of phone numbers with you at all times. People you can call at any time of the day or night in case the overwhelming urge hits. I tell my sponsees to comb their phone lists to find people they can call at the crack of dawn, and others they can call in the wee hours of the night. The chances are the latter is more likely and it gives your disease a chance to whisper in your ear, "*oh, it's late, you shouldn't bother anybody.*" The fact is, however, there are many people who would be there to keep you from breaking your abstinence if you reached out to them. Another possibility in the wee hours of the night are telephone meetings, which happen around the clock in many programs. It might be 3 in the morning for you, but it's mid-morning in England, which means there will be a meeting. By all means use it instead of turning to the food.

The key to battling this disease is not to just make that emergency list, but to be willing to commit to *using it* when the desire hits! The problem is that while part of my disease pushes me into the "overwhelming urge" territory, another part wants to convince me to _not_ make that phone call. "If you make that phone call," my disease whispers in my ear, "they might actually talk you out of it and then you don't get to eat!" If you want to be free of the food, however, making that call is exactly what you need to do, right? It was important for me to see that it was *the disease* telling me not to call. When I was able to see it as a fifth-columnist – an enemy trying to get me to defect to the other side – then it became a little easier to fight.

Another area in which people use the tool of Action Plan is, (and for some program people this is a dirty word): exercise. Exercise was nothing I was interested in when I first came into program, and probably for about the next ten years afterward. What I had to do at some point was to look at *why* the thought of exercise had such an unpleasant visceral effect on me. What I came to understand was that most of it was really old tapes.

As I mentioned, I was a fat kid. Ex-fat kids don't usually sit around regaling people with fond stories of their days in gym. As a kid, exercise meant one thing: gym class. I remember having one particular nasty gym teacher when I was growing up who seemed to take particular relish in berating me and making sure I was the center of ridicule. Later on in life, when I was one of the geeks in high school, the jocks were the ones I hated the most. At some point, I equated jocks and ridicule with exercise. Add to that a long history of trying to lose weight and exercise being one of the main tools you _had_ to do to lose that weight, and exercise was not something I did for fun. Exercise was a _task_, an assigned task, and an incredibly unpleasant one at that!

Fast-forward a number of years to my first marriage when my then wife and I were trying to lose weight. She had joined a gym and kept encouraging me to go. She kept telling me how much it improved her mood and attitude. After talking to a sponsor about my thoughts on exercise at that point, he got me to do some writing about my history with exercise, and that's when a lot of my feelings about it became fully formed and I was able to see them. Most importantly, I could see them as an adult in recovery, not as that hurt and embarrassed child.

Today, I _want_ to exercise for a number of reasons. First of all, exercise is for me a natural anti-depressant. When I get my cardio going and I really work out, it changes my overall mood for the day and even the day after that. It also increases my ever-decreasing metabolism a bit, and helps counteract a little bit of my calorie intake. However, I don't focus on that, as I do remember a time in my life after joining that gym that I spoke of, that I actually got into a bit of "exercise bulimia" for a while. The idea that I could work out as a way to eat more turned out to be a totally losing proposition. The fact is that you can wipe out hours of exercise with just one bad food choice afterwards, and more exercise often means more appetite as well.

Without getting overly spiritual on you, I feel today I have been given a gift and a new life. I feel that it's my responsibility to meet my Higher Power halfway with the things that I can do to maintain a body that has been through many food wars and escaped remarkably unscathed. There is a certain spiritual connection that can be had if you give exercise a chance.

My exercise of choice is running. For you, it might be something else. The key is to keep doing it regularly, and if possible, push yourself to do a little more every day. One of the things I had to do was to make exercise something I did at a regular time every day. When I didn't have a specific time carved out of my schedule every day, I would keep pushing it back until then it was too late.

If you are very overweight, in the beginning walking is great – sticking to level ground. Try then to extend the distance as you get healthier. The next step might be to try walking up and down hills, then possibly at a brisker pace. The key to repairing your body through exercise is getting your respiration and heart rate up to the point of it being slightly taxing. Swimming is another excellent form of exercise, as it utilizes almost all of the muscles in your body, and with less impact. Using the same regimen of slowly increasing distance and pace will soon have you feeling better, both physically and mentally.

One thing that helped me exercise longer was to find something to distract me, as running can be a bit boring and my mind needs something on which to focus. While some people like to listen to music, I don't find it distracting enough to allow me to "zone out" and forget I'm exercising. Now I listen to various spoken things, such as radio podcasts and O.A. speakers. A number of years ago, I started the L.A. Intergroup's "Virtual Speakers Bureau" which is still going strong. There are hundreds of O.A. speakers you can listen to while exercising your body and spirit. *(See the appendix at the end of this book for more details.)*

Writing

Some people use the tool of writing much better than I do. My old sponsor use to believe in writing every day, and he did it longhand. He had me write on the Steps longhand, which I found to be excruciatingly slow. I have heard people I respect, however, say that writing longhand really helps them slow down to concentrate better. Obviously, this is a matter of taste and my preference might very well not be your preference.

I do write, however, when I am emotionally stressed and need to move to "battle stations." What I came to understand about myself was that I was so out of touch with my emotions for so long, sometimes I had no idea how I was feeling at any given time. I spent years in therapy with therapists asking me the same

82

question over and over: "How do you *feel* about that. You've told me what you *think* about it, but how do you *feel* about it?" It was like speaking Martian to me.

For most of my life, I had used intellect at the expense of my emotions. In my family, I would hear things like "it's stupid to feel that way, don't feel that way." For years, I tried to intellectually override my emotions, especially when they were not always intellectually logical. I would tell myself, "it's stupid to feel that way, therefore I don't feel that way."

Lots of luck on that one.

What I had to realize was that often my emotions came out sounding like a ten year old. I could scold my ten year old and tell him not to feel that way, but the truth was that he was feeling the way he felt, because those were the feelings. What I had to come to understand was that I needed to let my ten year old have his say and not squash him down. Then I could acknowledge those feelings and then look to see how "we" (the inner ten year old and the adult John) could change them.

In those efforts, writing has been invaluable. Sometimes I find myself with just generalized anxiety that I cannot put my finger on. This is where writing often helps. There is a book for writers that describes something called "the morning pages." The theory is that you sit down every morning and write three pages a day no matter whether you want to or not. I have learned to do this kind of generalized "anxiety writing" to help me find an alternate way of calming myself – other than with food or alcohol. Nobody can withstand long periods of generalized anxiety without wanting to find something to calm those feelings.

Sometimes as I wrote these pages, the first half page says things like "I don't want to write, this is stupid," written over and over. As I continue, I can sometimes find some little thread onto which to pull. It's like finding a little thread on the shoulder of a suit jacket, and when you pull on it, the thread keeps unraveling until the sleeve falls off.

I will find myself writing, for example "Well, there was that thing that Jane said about me yesterday, but that didn't bother me." I'll then find myself starting to be my own self-examiner: "Well, if it didn't bother you, why are you writing about it now?" Often that is the beginning of the proverbial thread unraveling. Before I know it,

I see that some innocuous thing that, when I examined it head-on seemed fine, had instead disturbed my inner self. When I do this writing, it's like coming in the side door to a problem and suddenly that which was previously invisible becomes crystal clear.

Meetings

More than any other addiction, food addiction is about isolation. When I was a drinker, I spent the first part of my drinking around people in bars. It wasn't until I got deeper into my alcoholism that I started to drink at home. Recently, I heard another dually addicted person put his finger on what my situation had been: "Near the end of my drinking," he said. "I drank the way that I ate, in isolation." Turn on the TV, pull down the blinds, it's Miller time. This is even more true with compulsive eating.

There is another reason I need to go to meetings, and that is to "keep it green." Someone once said *"I'm not a slow learner, I'm a quick forgetter."* That statement definitely defines the nature of my disease and in this one area I have it really bad. When I think about my drinking days, I would regularly experience horrendous hangovers that would last until mid-afternoon. I would feel awful, be sweating and sometimes barely functional at work. Yet, when I left work, the idea of stopping to pick up a bottle seemed like a marvelous idea! This was only a few hours after I had been deathly ill. Now that is some quick forgetting! And the pain the disease of compulsive eating is even duller and easier to forget.

One of the ways that going to meetings combats the effects of isolation is putting my problems in perspective. It grounds out my reality. By myself, I can take the negative things in my life and totally blow them out of proportion. Then I go to a meeting and hear someone talk about being diagnosed with cancer, then someone else speaks about having to put their dog down and suddenly my problems are put into a better perspective.

I also believe in the concept of a *"group strength."* When I go to a strong meeting and hear numerous people talk about having all sorts of problems but not eating over them, it somehow adds to my strength. If they can go through the things they're going through without eating, why would my piddling stuff push me to eat?

84

I have a few pet peeves about things I hear about in meetings. One of those peeves is when meetings talk about having "positive pitches." While I do understand the concept of not turning a meeting into a dumping ground, I have always said that anyone can pitch anything – no matter how negative or horrible – as long as it ends with *"but I didn't eat over it."* If they do that, it's not a negative pitch in my book.

Along those lines I always like to relate what I was told by an old timer, who said "12 Step meetings are *not group therapy*. People didn't get into their car to come to the meeting saying 'Gee, I can't wait to hear how John is doing.' They come to get experience, strength and hope." Those words are in the preamble of almost every 12 Step program. Unless I'm the speaker, I'm there not to tell you my life story, but to be a positive influence on the meeting. What that little talk taught me was that if I didn't have any "experience, strength or hope" to share, perhaps I should just sit and listen. I'm not trying to be judgmental here, but I often see people who use meetings this way – as group therapy. Here's what's wrong with that – it doesn't work for them. Their lives do *not* get better. If it did, I'd chalk up my feelings as a personal peeve and shut up about it. But when I observe those people in a long-term way, they are talking about the same problems they were talking about two years ago! Why? Because nothing has changed in their lives – meaning *they* haven't changed. For them meetings and talk therapy is the answer and it's not. The Steps are the answer. As the old program adage goes: *"nothing changes if nothing changes."*

There is a definite arc of recovery that almost everyone goes through. When you first come to program, it's downright thrilling to hear people talking about the things you did and were deep dark secrets to you. Crazy things you did with food – things you were the only person on Earth to do (or so you thought) – turn out to be totally commonplace. When you hear people talking about the feelings you have had, you cannot help but want to chime in and become "part of the crowd" on such things. There's absolutely nothing wrong with that, it is part of the assimilation process. At some point a year or so down the line, if people continue to see the program as simply a place to come and talk about themselves and their problems, they stop growing. Yes, it feels good to talk about your problems and how beset with travails you are – but eating an ice cream sundae also felt good.

The reason those people stop growing is that they miss the glaring question dangling right before their eyes: "Okay, you've got problems... what are *you* going to do about them?" This is the point where people either pivot to the Steps and *do* something about their problems or they will stagnate, eventually relapse, and often leave program.

Every once in a while I will hear somebody going on about their troubles at a meeting and end with "... and that's why I binged last night." I always think to myself "Well heck, I know how to do that!" Where is the experience, strength and hope there? At the same time, in some of these cases, I think I understand why they do this. I've noticed that often the people who pitch like this at meetings don't have a sponsor. The exact things they need to talk out – with a sponsor one-on-one – they're bringing to the meeting and leaving in a steaming pile in the middle of the room. What I used to hear said a lot more at meetings was: *"Take your message to the meeting and your mess to your sponsor."*

The other important thing that was stressed to me early on was to get a home group. Have a group that you go to every week and where people will get to know you. The thing about having a home group is that people will quickly be able to see if you're upset and will be there to help. If you're new, take a service commitment. I decided to change my meetings up a few years ago and started going to a meeting I had attended and liked. The only problem was that I didn't know anybody. So what I did was to volunteer to be a greeter! Within a few weeks, I knew everyone and everyone knew me. You can't sit off in the corner and somehow absorb this program by osmosis. You need to be part of a group so that they can help you and in turn you can help others.

A warning about meetings

It's probably a little disconcerting to see the above header in a book promoting 12 Step recovery – but here goes anyway. 12 Step meetings – especially ones devoted to food – are the most democratic of institutions in the world. Anybody – and I do mean anybody – is provided their three minutes to speak. In A.A., newcomers and people newly sober are often given that terse A.A.

admonition: *"Take the cotton out of your ears and put it in your mouth."* (A.A. is not always as cuddly as 12 Step food programs.)

The point here is that with such a wide-open sharing policy, you can often hear some pretty off the wall things. If you are in your disease or struggling, you can also hear things that – if heeded – will reinforce your disease and *not* your recovery. I remember being in the middle of a slip when someone I know shared some really bizarre ideas about recovery and it fitted right in with my thinking at the time – which was based on my disease desperately trying to keep me from seeing how bad things really were. I asked her to be my sponsor with a really laissez-faire type of food plan. Guess what? Within a very short time she was gone, because it was a food plan based on her own diseased thinking. I cannot stress this caveat enough: *just because two people think the same thing doesn't mean it is right.* It could just be that more than one person is wrong (and in their disease) at the same time.

It's also important to remember that meetings are a big "one-room schoolhouse" with people at all levels of recovery attending the same meetings. Unlike A.A., there is also a portion of people attending 12 Step programs for food that are just "auditing" the 12 Step approach. The difference here is that if you've reached the point of considering A.A., you've *probably* got a problem with drinking. With food however, 12 Step programs are just one of many possible solutions for people with a weight problem. Some of these people might not be true compulsive eaters but have heard about 12 Step programs and come to meetings to see if it's for them. As a result, these people will sometimes share in a way different from those of us with a real problem. I have heard people speak about being able to take or leave food, take only a few bites – the kind of things spoken about in commercial weight loss program meetings. While there is nothing wrong with their view, I think for those of us with this disease, if we could do that, we would never have come to program.

If we are in the middle of a struggle with food, hearing things at meetings can cause us – or rather cause our disease to try to convince us – to consider moving in a different direction with the food. This can also happen if we hear of people being able to eat foods that we ourselves cannot eat with impunity. The voice of the disease – which can sound a bit like a whining child – will say to us

"Well, if _he_ can eat that thing, why can't I eat it and call myself abstinent?" The reason, of course, is that everyone is different when it comes to the food. I have sponsees that can eat what I cannot and vice versa.

There is a lot of diversity on how to work the program, and it's been deliberately designed to be flexible for a reason – people are different and need different approaches to find recovery. There are also some universal truths that you'll find. A program saying is: _"There are as many ways to work the program as there are people in it."_ While this might be true for people with one to about seven years (my 'magic number' is seven years), I find that the "road begins to narrow" with people with seven or more years of abstinence. Yes, they do have varied approaches, but they are not _that_ varied. Why? Simple Darwinian evolution: that which works is repeated, and that which does not work is not repeated. The people with odd ideas about recovery tend to drift off by about seven years. The people remaining are the ones you want to get close to. I have also noticed that the people who have the best recovery – the people who have what I want – don't tend to share at meetings very often. I think they learned something an old sponsor told me: _"People don't learn by talking, they learn by listening."_

One of the best phrases in the program is "stick with the winners." Look around at the people who are long-timers working a good program and start hanging out with them. One of my friends who attends O.A. meetings in Los Angeles says _"If you don't have ten years of abstinence, you're still a newcomer."_ That's a line that gets people a bit ticked off, but there is an underlying truth. It's not that there aren't people with perfectly good recovery with less than ten years of program, but I find the converse is not often true. You don't find people with ten years of recovery working some kind of wacky, slipshod program. If they've made it this long, they've probably found the right track.

When I lived back East, I could only imagine what true long-term recovery looked like. At one point in my early recovery, I tried to imitate it. I wanted to be an instant old-timer, but of course all that I actually had at that time was some weight loss. I was a real life example of "thin is not well." To imitate an old commercial "I wasn't an old timer, but I played one at meetings."

What I see in L.A. from the _real_ Old Timers are two things: first, they are human! They don't try to hide their foibles and when they tell their story, they talk openly about their character defects. They don't try to infer that their behavior became perfect on the day they walked into the rooms. They talk about how recovery and living a good 12 Step program is _work_, and how on any given day they may fail miserably at it. The other thing I see in the people I admire is that they are doing the same things today that they were doing the day they came into program. As they say "You can't stay clean on yesterday's shower."

Another thing I disagree with is the attempt by some meetings to ban the mentioning of specific foods. First of all, it never works. People in their shares want to mention the food, but following the rule results in them describing the item in much more detail than if they had simply mentioned it by name and moved on. Page 100 of the Big Book speaks about how we should no longer fear our substance. Food is no longer our master. It can't – well, it shouldn't – tell us how to run our meetings! If simply mentioning a food could push somebody "over the edge" into a binge, wasn't that person going to fail anyway? We have to come to terms with the fact that we cannot change the world to isolate and shelter us from our drug of choice (or more accurately our _drug of no choice_). After we leave a meeting, we might drive past 10 fast food joints, see 10 billboards for food products, and hear 10 commercials for food on the radio. This all goes to our being powerless over people, places and things. If there's one thing that a long time in program has taught me is that I only need to worry about my own abstinence; the next guy has his own Higher Power to do the worrying for him.

I will pass along the first piece of advice I got in my first week of my first program about meetings: "Come early, stay late, do service, and sit in the front so nobody can distract you." Also, let me tack on: keep an open mind at all meetings – remember what they say about 'contempt prior to investigation.' I try to say to myself as each meeting starts: "Okay, remember why you're here."

There's a reason why when they finish reading the Traditions, the words that are left ringing in your ears are: "_principles before personalities._" It's easy if you're new and coming off your substance to find people at meetings getting on your nerves. It's what happened to me when I first got sober. Everyone started bothering me. Then I started knowing too much about everyone and even though they might have been saying exactly what I needed to hear, I knew just a little too much of their back story. So when Joe said something profound (and exactly what I needed to hear), my cynical mind was saying "Yeah, but I know for a fact that you're having an affair with Phyllis over there" – and never heard a word of what he was saying. Forget about the fact that he had years of sobriety and I had a few weeks, I knew better. Guess what happened? One by one, I shut everyone out from helping me because my diseased brain found flaws in every one of them. After a time, *I* ended up drinking – not them! This was proof positive that it needs to be *"principles before personalities."* It's deathly important – to me – that I not start shooting the people in my own foxhole. I never know when I'm going to need them.

I remember one day I was at a meeting where we had a member who had – as they say in A.A. – *"problems other than alcohol."* This was a person who besides having our mutual disease had other mental problems. (An old sponsor used to say: "If you were crazy before you started drinking, the best we're going to be able to do is get you *back* to crazy.") At any rate, this fellow would often get up and give these rambling monologues that often didn't make much sense. One Sunday morning, I was tired and for whatever reason when he started talking I didn't have my usual judgment about him, which was usually then followed by me cynically tuning him out. On that morning, he said something... *brilliant!* What he said was *exactly* what I needed to hear concerning a problem I was having! The moral for me was I needed to keep an open mind about everybody. As Confucius says *"a wise man can always learn from a fool, but a fool can never learn from a wise man."* Now I try my best to keep an open mind and at the very least tell myself that I can listen to anything for three minutes. *Remember why you're there!*

Phone Meetings, Online Meetings and Podcasts

I have occasionally attended phone meetings (usually as a speaker) and have never "attended" an online meeting, but I believe both are indispensable for people in certain circumstances. If you live where there are no face-to-face meetings, or where there are very weak meetings, by all means use these meetings as a way to boost your program. They tend to be much like regular meetings in that there are strong attendees and then there are those who simply want to talk about their day. A meeting is what you take from it though, and I have always gotten something from the phone meetings of which I have been a part.

These meetings are also incredibly helpful if you get laid up. A friend from here in L.A. broke her leg a few months back and getting to meetings was all but impossible, but thanks to phone meetings, she was able to get her "booster shot" of meetings.

Online meetings are meetings that run in real time, but involve reading and typing of "dialog", so it is something of an acquired taste for some. Older folks such as myself – especially if they are blessed with face-to-face meetings in their area – tend to not find them as helpful.

One thing I do counsel against is using phone or online meetings as a *substitute* for face-to-face meetings. Remember, this is a disease of isolation, and there will be a tendency to want to just stay at home and listen or type. Unless you cannot physically make it to a face-to-face meeting, it should not be the default meeting type you attend. Recovery is about breaking the isolation. Also, if you are going through a particularly bad time when there might not be a scheduled meeting, try to get together with a fellow member for coffee. Remember, that whenever two program people are together, there is a meeting.

Another possible way to boost your program is through podcasts. In 2007, the L.A. Intergroup of O.A. founded the first such podcast, "*The Virtual Speakers' Bureau*," Being a friend of members of that Intergroup Board, and because of my technical abilities, I was instrumental in bringing this service live and it's by far the thing of which I am most proud in my time around 12 Step programs. The O.A.LAIG podcasts have grown to four different feeds as of this writing and boasts over 60,000 downloads a month. People from all over the world download the podcasts, which contain many people with 20, 30 and even 40 years of abstinence. They can be accessed via the L.A. Intergroup website (www.oalaig.org) or also via podcast downloaders such as iTunes. Simply search for "Overeaters Anonymous" and you'll find them.

A few years after the L.A. Intergroup started posting podcasts, the O.A. World Service Office began offering podcasts of its own, and now a number of different O.A. Intergroups and Regions have podcasts – or at least downloadable MP3 files. There are also podcasts available from other 12 Step food programs. An Internet search should give you more information on those podcasts.

The great thing about podcasts is that they are totally portable. Once you have downloaded them in your iPod, phone, or whatever device you choose to use, you can listen to them anywhere and at any time. It can be three in the morning, and a thousand miles from any Internet connection, and you can still hear great O.A. recovery. The phrase "You're never alone" is true now more than ever.

The Telephone as a Tool

One of the Tools in food programs is the telephone. For years, these programs have stressed using the phone as a way to break out of our isolation. When I have a sponsee that is an isolator, I will ask that he talk to three fellow members a day via the phone. Notice that I did not say "make three phone calls a day," because that might very well mean getting an answering machine or voicemail. I cannot tell you how many times I've listened to my voicemail and heard "Hi John, this is so-and-so, I'm just making my outreach calls. Bye." My guess is that person has a certain amount of calls his or her sponsor wants made each day, and so this is the process. But what has really been achieved? In the end, not much. Talking to another member, however, is a meeting between meetings.

There is a wonderful thing about setting this goal this way – *talking* to three people a day. In the beginning, it means making more than three calls until you actually speak to a live person, but it will later result in you making *fewer* calls. Why? Once you start talking to people on a regular basis, *they* will then start calling *you*. You will be surprised at how many close friends you will end up with that started as an outreach call to a stranger.

If you detest the idea of calling someone cold, why not start by talking to them at a meeting and saying "Hi, my name is John, and I need to call people every day. Do you mind if I call you?" This way, the person will be able to put a face to your name – and vice versa.

A newer version of this tool is texting. I know a number of people who use texting – not as a substitute for the telephone – but as a way to reach out when things get tough. Someone spoke recently of having to be in a big company meeting for hours and there were loads of donuts, which people were eating because the meeting was running long and everyone was hungry. Thanks to our new technology, she was able to text a number of her program friends and scream – not with her voice, but with her fingers. Sometimes, just venting about how tough a food situation you are in is enough to dissipate the anxiety.

Literature

As is said, program literature can be a "meeting between meetings." Moreover, it can remove me from a possible "brain loop" and provide a much-needed jog into different thinking. For me, the main pieces of literature I use daily are the A.A. Big Book and both the A.A. 12 & 12 and the O.A. 12 & 12. I have, at different times in my life, started my day with a reading from one of the daily readers (*"For Today"*, for example). Having some new thought put into my head daily is a way to open my mind to thoughts that might not otherwise be there. Also, by starting your day with some kind of reading, you are building the "muscle" of daily meditative work.

In terms of pamphlets, if you are in O.A., I would suggest you read *"Before You Take That First Compulsive Bite"* and *"A Commitment to Abstinence."* These are invaluable for newcomers to read because they stress how important it is to make abstinence the most important thing in their lives. O.A. members also can subscribe to *"Lifeline,"* the program's 10 times a year magazine. If you live in an area without many meetings and cannot access the various podcasts, *"Lifeline"* might help a lot.

One last piece of literature I cannot recommend enough is an A.A. pamphlet called *"A Member's Eye View of Alcoholics Anonymous."* This is the transcript of a talk from an A.A. member from Los Angeles who also happened to be a therapist. It was given to a graduating class of UCLA students who were going on to become addiction counselors. In it, he describes A.A. and the 12 Step process of recovery to people who were not addicts, and in a much more modern style. While there isn't anything in the pamphlet that isn't covered in the Big Book and A.A. 12 & 12, it explains it in a very forthright and clear manner that I find helpful.

It is divorced from that slightly archaic prose in which the Big Book and 12 & 12 are written.

Summing up so far

These first chapters focused on the concept of getting – or restoring – your abstinence. The first three Steps, along with the help of the Tools, are the centerpiece of getting this far. If you are still having problems keeping food from being an addiction in your life, take some time to re-read the sections on understanding the disease and on powerlessness.

The most important thing is to begin to perceive your disease as separate from *you*. Being able to identify the "voice" of the disease – not in the tone, but in the things it says – is the key to being able to fight it. Remember, you wouldn't be doing all of this 12 Step work if you truly wanted to continue on the path of destructive eating. As I've said, when that disease "salesman" makes the sale, he also wants to convince you that the urge to eat was your idea – and then the guilt sets in.

How about trying a different tactic? I know some people who give their disease a name and then respond to it whenever it tries to whisper something in their ear. One person calls her disease "Fred" and when the urge hits her she says, "Thanks for the suggestion Fred, but I think I'll just eat that abstinent lunch instead of that ice cream you're pointing me towards."

It may sound a little strange, but the point is that she has found a way to battle the disease as an enemy attacking her constantly, not as a "change of mind" or "momentary lapse of willpower."

After all, we *do* have a disease and it's trying to kill us. We just can't let it try to convince us that it would be a suicide.

Chapter 7 – Steps 4 & 5: Moving out of neutral

Step 4: "Made a searching and fearless moral inventory of ourselves."

The first three Steps are often called "the give up Steps." It is through the process of surrender embodied in these beginning Steps that recovery begins to take root. While Steps 3 and 4 are adjacent in a number sequence sense, there is – in actuality – a chasm between them.

The first three Steps, along with the Tools (and a healthy dose of surrender) should have been sufficient to help the average compulsive eater to "put down the food." Putting the food down alone is only a small part of the process. We must now work on our character defects, as these are the "weak links" that our disease will try to use to get back into our lives. We must address and begin to change these behaviors or it's only a matter of time before everything falls apart.

Everyone I have known who relapsed after a significant amount of time in program had one significant thing in common: they hadn't continued to work on their program. Most often they hadn't done a 4th Step (along with the subsequent amends), or did a very cursory 4th Step and ceased the digging and self-examination soon afterwards. That kind of "half measure" gave their disease the inroad it needed. Even though we may be in recovery, our disease is constantly scouring the situation for a new way back in.

When doctors prescribe antibiotics to patients, they always do so with a specific regimen. The patients are told to continue taking the full regimen, even though they may feel better long before the antibiotics run out. The same is true with recovery in the Steps. Having done the work of surrender and broken the immediate pull of the addiction, it's easy to delude ourselves into thinking we are better long before we have any kind of long lasting recovery. My early story was a perfect example of that. I didn't continue to do the work, and I paid the price for it.

Fear of the 4th Step

The 4th Step says *"Made a searching and fearless moral inventory of ourselves."* I mention the exact wording because it seems to me that a lot of people misread this as *"Write a treatise the size of a classic Russian novel about every little thing that has ever bothered you, every slight ever done to you and especially any action – no matter how small – of less than sterling character you may have done in your entire life. While you're at it, include any <u>thoughts</u> that were never translated into action."*

There appears to be many reasons why people put off writing a 4th Step. However, fear seems to be underlying any and all reasons for delaying this Step. Let's examine the reality of this fear.

Memories? They can't hurt you. Dredging up the past might bring back some painful memories, but again these are memories you find while going through your cluttered old house of a brain and they need to be thrown out – or neutralized at the very least. The thing to realize about this process is that it is front-loaded with pain, but you need to trust it. In the end, when that thousand pound weight is off your shoulders, the reason for doing all this work will make sense.

Another source of fear of a 4th Step concerns envisioning having to share it with another human being. Let me remind you that sharing it is not the 4th Step, that's the 5th Step! I counsel all of my sponsees: *"There is no such thing as the FourthFifth Step. There's a Fourth Step and a Fifth Step. They are two discrete Steps and are separate for a reason."*

The 4th Step is about getting all of this stuff out onto paper for <u>you</u> to read and contemplate. Don't spend a moment thinking about or worrying about with whom you will share it later. That's not important right now. You do <u>not</u> have to give it to your sponsor. You can decide to give it to a clergyman, a therapist (I did one of those), or somebody not even in program (although having a person familiar with the 12 Step process would be helpful). If you are going to be censoring what comes out on your 4th Step because you've got one eye on the 5th Step, you're doing it wrong!

If after all of this, you're still paralyzed with fear about starting, take a breath and look backward at Step 3. Have you really made a decision to turn your will and life over to a power (or process) greater than yourself? A universal axiom in 12 Step programs is that if you're having trouble with a Step, then maybe you didn't fully complete the one before it. Whether you believe in an established type of Higher Power or you're just holding on to the group and the program as your version of a Higher Power, it comes down to one thing: *faith*. Trust that we're not going to steer you wrong. We're not lying when we tell you that at the end of this process, *you will feel better!*

Another reason for delay is the thought that you'll be writing that novel I spoke of earlier. The more time in program I have, the more I see that what I heard over and over when I first came into program is right: *moderation in everything*. When push comes to shove, I tell my sponsees to seize on the Nike version of the 12 Steps: *"Just Do It."*

Don't worry about it being totally comprehensive and complete. If you are, as I am, planning on being around here for the long term, you'll be doing more than one 4th Step anyway! If there is one thing I can guarantee you, is that even if you have written the 4th step novel of our generation, the moment you've given away your 5th Step, you'll think of something you missed.

Why do long-timers do multiple 4th Steps, you may ask. Isn't a 4th Step, followed by a daily 10th Step enough? In the early days, I thought so, but here's the truth about long term recovery in 12 Step programs: you keep "peeling the onion" deeper and deeper. Things I hadn't even thought of as wrong when I did my first 4th Step ended up on subsequent 4th Steps. As I often joke, "While I can appreciate learning more as I peel the onion, I can't help but feel they're making more onion on me." The fact is that the road gets narrower and we begin to be willing to dig deeper.

One last suggestion: don't re-write your 4th Steps! If you do a second inventory, it should only contain the things you forgot, uncovered, or did since your last 4th Step. Don't reinvent the wheel!

Doing a 4th Step

There are loads of different ways of doing a 4th Step, and let me take a moment to talk about some of them. When I was in a different program, I once did a 4th Step that involved answering something like 170 different questions. Some of these questions helped jog my memory, but mostly it felt like taking a test. And just like taking a test, as soon as I was done doing that 4th Step, it was out of my consciousness.

There are also 4th Step Workbooks, like the one O.A. puts out. While it might be good to take a look through them to see what kinds of things one might put down on a 4th Step, I believe it still comes down to one important concept: "What's eating _you_?" As the old program saying goes: "We eat over what's eating us," I couldn't agree more. The thing that might be eating away at you might be inconsequential to me. Things listed in various workbooks are probably real things that bothered the people who wrote them – but not necessarily things that bother you. That's what makes a 4th Step so individual.

I hate to be conventional, but I think the classic three column A.A. Inventory found on page 65 of the Big Book is the one that works best. Many people add to that inventory an additional column that concerns "what's my part in it?" or "what is the core character defect that drives this?" I think this a very good idea. I know people who use a spreadsheet program to do this, which is utilizing the technology we now possess. The idea of being able to look across at that list, and then be able to sort such a list based on that last column is key to seeing the _patterns_ throughout our lives and the character defects that drove them.

Let me take a moment here to say something about the phrase "character defects." Like many of the phrases we see in the Big Book, this one tends to reflect the times in which the writers lived. There is a certain judgment folded into the phrase "character defect" that bothers me quite a bit. What these were — when you get right down to it – were "defense mechanisms." Many of us grew in abnormal circumstances and these "defense mechanisms" were the normal reaction to an abnormal situation. The problem is, of course, that their usefulness and effectiveness have long ago waned and now these same mechanisms that at one time helped us, now cause us immeasurable harm.

Many people in the 12 Step community use a variety of worksheets based on the Big Book 4th Step. Many of these sprang from "Joe and Charlie" workshops. Joe and Charlie were two A.A. long-timers (the "Joe" was actually two different men named Joe over the years) who dissected the Big Book and came up with a systematic method for working the Steps.

In the newer versions of 4th Steps, they add a final column on the right-hand side. It's called various things, such as "Core Character Defects", or "What's My Part in This" or various other versions of the same thought. The point is that this final column is the extension to the "affects my" column and is the link to the 6th and 7th Steps. Being able to look at this list of character defects is as important in relating to Steps 6 and 7 as the first column is in relating to the later 8 and 9 Amends Steps. Again, there is a flow to the Steps if done correctly and here we can "follow the path" much more closely.

To that end, I'm a big fan of the forms that Lawrie C. from Winnipeg, Canada has posted. They were originally designed by Blaine, also from Winnipeg. In addition to being exemplary in their construction, they are also geared to compulsive eaters rather than alcoholics. They can be found at: www.oabigbook.info and can be downloaded and printed at home. There are three main subjects: resentments, fears and sex.

Resentments

At the core of most resentments is – surprise – anger. Often, this is an emotion that we men have no trouble accessing. I have said that for most men new to recovery, there are two emotions: angry and about to get angry. It is the default male emotion. Why? I would guess because it's the "macho" emotion we are more ready to admit to our fellows and ourselves. Less "macho" emotions like hurt, fear, etc. are often seen as less in tune with the male psyche. The thing to understand is that anger is actually a *secondary* emotion – it always sits on top of other emotions like fear and hurt.

For other people, however, getting in touch with anger might not be so easy. For some, anger was considered a less than desirable emotion, and as a result those people were taught to suppress them. Suppressing any emotion is like playing "whack-a-mole" – you're not really eliminating it, just inviting it to come out in some other way. For many, stifling anger means turning to depression. As has been said, "depression is anger turned inward,"

The other thing about anger and resentment is that it provides us with all kinds of excuses for our personal failings. One of my favorite stories in the Big Book is called *"Freedom from Bondage,"* It is near the end of the book, but has been around since the Second Edition and was written by one of the early female members of A.A. In it, she talks about the resentment she had with her mother: *"[This resentment]... was 25 years old. I had fed it, fanned it, and nurtured it as one might a delicate child, and it had become as much a part of me as my breathing. It had provided me with excuses for my lack of education, my marital failures, personal failures, inadequacy, and of course, my alcoholism and, though I really thought I had been willing to part with it, now I knew I was reluctant to let it go."*

It actually is a big part of our self-realization to admit to ourselves that sometimes we don't *want* to let go of negative things like that resentment and other character defects we find later. It's okay because it's part of human nature. At the same time, it's important to realize that we _do_ have to let them go. While holding on to such familiar feelings might be comforting these are also the stones we cling to while we're drowning.

Concerning the 4th Step list itself: the two leftmost columns, of course, are the list of people we resent or have resented, and the reason we resent them. My sponsor suggested to me – and I agree – that the best thing to do is just start listing people. Don't worry about the things they *did* right now, just start filling out the list, top to bottom. When you finally get to the point where you can't think of anyone else, *then* start going across to the next column and write about the things that caused the resentment. If you're like me, as you're doing that, you'll think of more people and start adding to the list. Don't worry, it's fine to do it this way. Being comprehensive is much more important than being tied to the form taken.

As you enter the "affects my" area, you'll begin to see the patterns of how we have very often not "acted" in life, but instead simply "_re_acted." Often this revolves around that little five year old that is still up in the rafters of our heads. The petulant child that didn't like that he wasn't recognized for his efforts, or had his desires ignored in favor of someone else. This is the kind of thing entered here.

The final column has to do with our part in it. Where was I selfish, self-seeking, dishonest, or fearful? Now, there is the fact that there are certain resentments for which we will have no part in (if, for example, we were abused – physically or sexually – as children). Then we can leave that area blank. Be careful not to whitewash events though, as these will be the kinds of things that might fester in our brains and later be the cause of us going out and eating. For example, was my part in abusive relationships later in life due to me picking the same type of partner over and over?

Fears

I am of the belief that if you drill down on almost all of our problems, fear is at the heart of them. As has often been said in meetings: "There are only two kinds of fear that cover every other fear. They are fear of not getting what we want, or fear of losing something we already have." Amen.

In the Fear Inventory, it's important to not only write about what each fear is, but *why* you have the fear. Digging down and understanding why that fear is there will often help you overcome it. The final lifting of fear comes in the form of the rewards of completing this 12 Step process – the finding of some kind of faith in a power greater than ourselves.

Sex

We'll be dealing with sex in an entire chapter later in this book, but for now, it's important to talk about the place sex has within the inventory process. For the most part, it has to do with our behavior and how it negatively impacted others.

For some, this involves infidelity. For others, it involves improperly using sex as a motivator to manipulate others. Sometimes it involves "luring" people into sex with the promise of a love that didn't exist. If something involves sex and makes you feel bad when you think about it, it belongs on the inventory.

Some final thoughts on a 4th Step

I was given an important piece of advice before embarking on my first 4th Step: Lose the rationalization and self-justification. While some of us unnecessarily flagellate ourselves for our humanness, others try to sweep their wrong doings under the rug via the wonderful tools of rationalization and justification. As it says in "Freedom from Bondage," *"rationalization is giving a socially acceptable reason for socially unacceptable behavior, and socially unacceptable behavior is a form of insanity."*

Or as I heard said at a meeting once: "I judged myself by my intentions while others judge me by my actions."

Step 5 – Giving it all Away

Step 5: "Admitted to God, to ourselves, and to another human being the exact nature of our wrongs."

As I said, I'm a big believer in the idea that you do not have to read your 5th Step to a sponsor. There's nothing written anywhere that says this, although I think a lot of people in program think it is the case. A sponsor might often be the logical person with whom to do a 5th Step, but if doing it with him or her will in any way make you uncomfortable or censor your 4th Step – don't do it! If any sponsor says you do have to do it with him/her, ask exactly where that is written (the Big Book doesn't even mention sponsors!). You can do a 5th Step with a clergyman, a therapist, or anyone else with whom you'd feel at ease.

As they say: "You're only as sick as your secrets." I thought my sponsor would hear my secrets and get sick. Not only did that *not* happen, but for every horrible thing I talked about, he came back with "You think *that's* bad..." as he told me something he had done that was even worse! I started to get a resentment about it. At one point, I joked: "Hey! This isn't 'Can you top this?' you know!" What I really resented, of course, was that he was puncturing my terminal uniqueness. There is something of a perverse ego flip of needing to be the <u>worst</u> piece of crap in the room.

When I finished my first Fifth Step, I walked on air when leaving. I could now walk down the street and look people in the eye. For the first time in many, many years, my insides again matched my outsides. It was a new beginning.

If at all possible, try to do your 5th Step in one sitting. If you've written a particularly long 4th Step, of course this might not be possible. However, when you're done, the Big Book recommends – and I agree – trying to take some time to reflect on what you've done. You've finished unloading the past. Whatever comes from this day forward, hopefully you'll be doing so with new eyes and a life that includes the 12 Steps. That's not to say you won't make mistakes and possibly start entries in your next 4th Step, but with any luck, they won't be so destructive.

One last note about a custom some people have: burning your 4th Step when you're done. There's nothing wrong with doing this, but make sure you have a list of the people on that 4th Step first, as it will be the basis for your later 8th Step!

Chapter 8 – Steps 6 & 7: We are not perfect after all

Step 6: "Were entirely ready to have God remove all these defects of character."

"Entirely" and *"all"* are the problem words in the Sixth Step. This concept demands some absolutes to which many of us have trouble adhering. As I mentioned earlier, this is one of those places where it might be necessary to take a few steps backward. If we have been able to have faith in the process, we will have faith that these defects, at least the ones we don't want to let go of, will be replaced with better coping mechanisms. If we can't find a way to be ready to embrace the "entirely" and "all" concepts, we might think about how well we have done Steps One through Five.

In many ways, the two most overlooked Steps are Six and Seven – yet, they are among the most vital of Steps for growth and continued recovery. To go back to the disease paradigm I used earlier, think of your character defects as the antibodies the disease of compulsive eating uses to fight against recovery.

Let me reiterate what I said earlier about the phrase "character defects." I will continue to use it here, because it's become the standard way of describing them in 12 Step programs, but I'm not a big fan of the phrase. It was born in an earlier time, and is only slightly removed from a highly moralistic "good vs. evil" type of thinking. The word "defect" denotes a flaw, and in turn makes some of us think of ourselves as defect_ive_.

What are commonly known as "character defects" started out as defense mechanisms from a dysfunctional family situation during childhood or adolescence. While they were useful to us at one time, they have become what some prefer to call "character liabilities," I think this term best describes them, but without any inherent judgment folded in.

Many of us grew up in abnormal households, often very dysfunctional ones. As a result, we developed coping mechanisms that worked for us in those abnormal environments. So, the phrase "defense mechanisms" is a good one, in that they often "defended" us from some of that craziness – or at least lessened the pain a bit.

In the battle of life, these "defense mechanisms" are no longer defenders, and more often than not they are working against us. In terms of the words "defense" and "offense," they've gone over to the other side.

We weren't born broken. Ours was often a natural reaction to a difficult situation. One of my favorite films was about a war crimes trial called "Breaker Morant," In it, the defense lawyer says: *"The barbarities of war are seldom committed by abnormal men. The tragedy of war is that these horrors are committed by normal men in abnormal situations."* To a (much) lesser extent, this was our situation growing up. We were normal kids that developed in an abnormal environment, and thus have some strange coping mechanisms that we must now *un*learn.

In this chapter, in addition to looking at the Steps involved, we'll also examine some of the major "character defects" and see how they can affect our ability to recover.

On the surface, many of us are ready to have our *most troublesome* defects removed. It is some of the other, more subtle, ones to which we might have found a fond attachment. In other cases, it may take years of growth to even realize that some of the character traits we had believed were just traits might also be character defects. This is one of those areas where our growth is gradual – like peeling that onion. Later on in recovery, we often realize things we had originally categorized as "strengths" were actually working against us.

The key here is to be willing to let go of *all* of them, "root and branch," as it says in "Bill's Story." There is an irony that men and women who come to program often have little or no faith in the formal, religious definition of the word. Working the Steps, however, requires developing faith – in increasing frequency – at least in the Step process itself.

First, there is the faith in believing us when we tell you that once you've accepted powerlessness, someone else might know better than you about conquering your disease. Then when we tell you that writing down the things of which you are most ashamed and admitting them to another human being will make you feel better. Hopefully, if you have done these things, the concept of faith is building because you are able to see with your own eyes that we were right. Now that we have reached this Step, we again ask for your faith and trust that letting go of all of your defects is the way to a happier, more rewarding life. These "defense mechanisms", you will begin to realize, are no longer needed. They have either already been, or will be, supplanted by new and more healthy – and most importantly, more *effective* – coping strategies. Taking these incremental leaps of faith are the key – to act our way into right thinking instead of the other way around.

Character Defects: the Disease's Arsenal

When I look at the list of my character defects, there are two main ones from which almost all of the others sprout: Immaturity and Narcissism (often referred to as "self-centeredness" in the Big Book).

Immaturity

At the core of our disease is a certain personality type. In A.A., they often call it "the alcoholic personality." The more I have observed it, the more I'm convinced it's simply an *immature* personality. In my case, and in the case of many people I have worked with in program, I think this is a matter of too much "mommy love" and not enough "daddy love."

That "mommy love", as I mentioned earlier, was important in our early development, building confidence and a healthy self. Its one drawback was to give us a slightly unhealthy perspective about our *"specialness,"* At some point, there needs to be a counter-balancing force that helps us see ourselves and our place in the world in an objective way. My mother told me over and over just how special and terrific I was – to the point that I actually believed it.

One of my favorite posters shows a snowflake with the caption: "You are unique, like a snowflake! *Like every other snowflake.*" The point here being, by a certain age I needed a little less of what she was doling out as "mommy love," and a little more reality based "daddy love." The operative word here, by the way, still being "love."

Those lacking "daddy love" tend to be missing the vital lessons needed to make a good, mature, well-balanced adult. One of the most important lessons being that at some point we have to take responsibility for our actions and quit blaming everyone and everything for our own personal failings. Yes we are special, but specialness alone gets you nowhere. Specialness and hard work, however, can make for extraordinary accomplishments. These are statements one can associate with "daddy love."

All of the primary methods our disease uses against us prey mainly on our immaturity. There's a reason we read about looking for "the easier, softer way" in "How It Works" – because in most compulsive eaters' immature brains is someone looking for the easy way out. This is not a trait consigned to compulsive eaters alone. There's a billion dollar industry out there peddling an almost infinite number of "easier, softer ways" to problem eaters. The reality is that if any of those ways really worked, it would eliminate the competition and become _the_ way to battle problem eating. To lift a line from the Big Book: "*science may one day accomplish this, but it hasn't done so yet.*"

I remember one time reminding a sponsee of the sentence in "More About Alcoholism" that says (in food terms): "*It is the great desire of every [compulsive eater] to somehow [eat] like a normal person.*" To which he said, "no... we really don't want to eat like normal eaters. We want to eat the way we want to eat and have no adverse effects." I thought about it and he was absolutely right. Normal eaters will take one bite of a piece of cake and say "oh... that's too rich." What? I don't understand the phrase "too rich" in any possible definition of the word "rich,"

The specific insanity of the disease is amazing to me. I am a person pretty well-grounded in reality in most areas, just not when it comes to food. If I said to myself "I want to hit the lottery every night... not for a lot, just a few thousand dollars," I would have no trouble knowing that was absurd. Yet there is still a small part of me – all these years into recovery – that secretly hopes that one day I will figure out that magic way to eat the way I want and not gain weight. After all, I'm going to a 12 Step program, aren't I – that should be the reward! Luckily when any thought like that comes up, I can just smile at it and see the insanity that I could not see before program.

Another aspect where my disease attacks me via my immaturity is through my denial and dishonesty about my food. As I said previously, the ability to BS myself – and others – is one of the disease's most potent weapons it can use against me. It's that much harder when dealing with a food addiction, because it is not very easy to deny you're in a slip in A.A. or N.A. The single most difficult thing for a true compulsive eater to do is be 100% honest about his/her food – both with him/herself and with a sponsor.

We all have certain foods or behaviors that we don't want to give up, and we try to convince ourselves we can "handle them." No matter how many times we "dance with the devil" with those foods and behaviors, they inevitably come back to bite us. We give them up for a while and then take them back, often putting "strict" parameters on how much or how often we can eat them. With these newly imposed parameters, *this time will be different* with these foods. We might even have limited success for a while. The slow slide, however, eventually comes. The disease's way of making this work is to make that "slide" back to eating those foods imperceptible enough that we cannot see the progression until it's too late.

The important thing is to be able to look at the big picture of the food. Is it keeping me from growing because I'm playing with it and not allowing myself to have a good, clean abstinence? *There is a difference between clean abstinence and controlled eating.* When I am dabbling with foods that I know I "can't handle," I am not living with a clean abstinence, but rather I'm trying to control my food. More importantly, the act of doing this controlled eating takes a lot of time and effort – time and effort I could use more effectively by learning how to grow up.

The disease often tries to use this immature part of myself to turn me against the program that is trying to save my life. I know at one point in my recovery, I started to try to rebel against the program. *"Who are these people telling me how I should live and what I should eat?"* That's what I would say to myself. The answer was obvious: nobody is saying for a moment I _have_ to do anything! As is often said in program, "we'll refund your misery whenever you decide to leave." One sponsor was asked by a sponsee "How long do I have to do all this stuff?" The sponsor replied, "You only _have_ to do all this stuff until you _want_ to do all this stuff, and then you don't _have_ to do this stuff at all anymore."

The disease's trump card would be if it could convince me that program doesn't work – or at least doesn't work for me. If this happens, then I've cut off my last avenue for recovery. After that, I'm truly headed down the road to destruction.

My disease uses my immaturity to cause my selective memory to kick in. I start to think of the foods that were killing me in terms I used when I was a kid: "goodies" and "comfort food." It has the remarkable ability to blank out all of the painful memories I had around the food and its effects on me. It's the disease again trying to hold up that balance sheet with all of the plusses of recovery whited out! It wants me to believe that somehow, some way, I can get something for nothing. When it comes to recovery though – and yes, another food reference – *there is no such thing as a free lunch*.

At an O.A. workshop a few years back, the leader asked people to yell out words associated with abstinence. You know what one word came up more than any other word? "Deprivation." Mostly these were people in the middle of slips, so this is where they were coming from. Consider if I changed that question to "living without gambling." Would the word "deprivation" really pop into our minds? Probably not, unless we are also compulsive gamblers. If abstinence is really about eating a healthy diet that nourishes our bodies, why would that be considered deprivation? It is not, unless we have an unhealthy relationship with food – or our disease is screaming lies in our ears.

Narcissism, Ego and Self-centeredness

Narcissism, ego and self-centeredness are three of my larger – and less desirable – character liabilities. Like many people I know in program, I was raised by immature parents who were themselves narcissists. In terms of maturity, I did not have good role models to show me how I should comport myself as a mature adult as I grew up. Additionally, as narcissists, they passed that trait down to me. It is said that often children of narcissists tend to become narcissists themselves – and there are a number of very good books written about this.

One of the things I had to admit about myself – mostly through various inventories – was just how much I lived in the "whirlpool of self." I also call it the "*prison* of self," which is a more accurate description. Every event that intersected my life was somehow personally connected to me or my life – or so I believed. As a result, I took so many things so personally, amplifying those problems exponentially. When someone cut me off in traffic, I was doubly angry about the act, because I somehow saw it as a personal affront. No... it really wasn't personal. The guy was just clueless. As a friend said to me once: *"Never attribute to maliciousness that which can more likely be attributed to cluelessness."*

The other thing about such affronts is that they came from an aggrandized view of myself in the world. *"Don't they know who I am?"* – that phrase would be the sub-conscious thought feeding the anger. This was another part of my warped brain: *I'm special*. The rules don't apply to me. I have good reasons for breaking the rules. Everyone else has to play by those rules or I get angry, mind you, but *I* am the special case.

When I was newly sober, I had a particularly warped self-view. I had a profound superiority complex. I would actually say this out loud: "Most people with superiority complexes have them as masks for inferiority complexes, but in my case I'm actually just superior." What a jerk! After a number of years in program and with the help of therapy I realized the answer: what was *really* at the bottom of all of this was the profound fear that I wasn't as good as you. To compensate, I had to puff up my ego – if for no other reason than to try to convince myself I was okay. In the end, the sad, boring truth was what I had feared: my superiority complex *was* masking an inferiority complex.

When you scratch the surface on almost all of the character liabilities having to do with ego and self-centeredness, they point back to fear. Fear that we're not good enough, fear we won't be recognized for our efforts, fear of... well, I could go on forever. One of the true leaps in growth came when I realized I'm exactly the person I'm supposed to be – and the person my Higher Power wants me to be.

The most dangerous trait of self-centeredness though comes from one thing: *terminal uniqueness*. There was always this belief in me when I was younger that I was smart – and usually smarter than almost everyone else. When I was in high school, I found out that my intelligence was rated in the top 1 percentile. This was, in retrospect, a very dangerous thing for me to know. It meant to me – and my warped brain – that if I was in a room with 100 people, chances were that I was the smartest one in the room. That knowledge did something that was incredibly counter-productive in my life – it made me unteachable when it came to important life lessons. No matter what mistake I would hear about others making, it certainly didn't pertain to _me_. _I_ would never make that mistake because I was smarter. What I did not grasp was that they're called mistakes for a reason. Nobody sets out to make mistakes!

If you told me that a stove in the room was hot and that I shouldn't touch it, I would have to touch it – and burn myself slightly – just to see. What I couldn't understand was said best in an old saying: _"Intelligent people learn from their mistakes, but wise people learn from other people's mistakes."_

What makes this terminal uniqueness especially dangerous, as it applies to my disease, is that I stop being teachable. I cannot use what many see as the main strength of going to meetings: to hear how to not eat, a day at a time. If I think I'm so much smarter than the other people in the rooms, I cannot form the thought: "if it can happen to them, it can happen to me – I'd better listen to what they're saying."

I've known a number of people in program over the years that are dead as the direct result of this disease. They're not "having a bad time," not "slipping," their food isn't "sloppy" — they're _dead_. The scary thing about this is that these people I am talking about were all people who were abstinent at one point – some for a long time – and then they gave it away. Not one of them said, "Screw it, I'm going to eat myself to death." They all just started to let their program slip in some small way. Here's where I am thankful I lost my terminal uniqueness, because what I think about when I am reminded of this is this: _if they can end up dead, I can end up dead._

Another part of my ego is my defiance. In psychology I have what is known as an oppositional-defiant personality. That means if you tell me when I leave a place I have to take a left, I'm taking a right – even if it's off a cliff. When I scratched beneath the surface of that character trait, I realized I was terrified of being just one of the group. There was a two-fold problem with that: one, I had a need to feel special. Another part of it was that deep-down I didn't feel I could compare favorably to others, so I wanted to set myself apart deliberately, so nobody could see how much less than everyone else I was. As I said before, everything comes down to fear, in one form or another.

Another part of my ego and self-centeredness was paranoia. I came from a family that bred this into us. We were taught to be on guard, that people were out to get you. The truth was, sadly, nothing like that. I say sadly because even in my self-delusional belief in persecution, I aggrandized my importance in peoples' lives. As I said earlier: *"What would depress me most about what people think about me is how little people think about me."*

Control Issues

Another defect that often springs from self-centeredness and ego is what is known today by the blanket phrase: "control issues." Often people who are smart think they know best about everything. A lot of times they *do* know things better than others. The trouble is when they go from mentioning a problem that could be made better by a suggested change to being insistent that the other person (or persons) do it the way *they* think is best. It's important to remember that what might be perfect for you might not be perfect for another. As someone once said: *"other people are not imperfect versions of you."*

To be honest, this is one of the defects with which I battle the most. Having come from a "child of alcoholic" background, I got very good at a young age at identifying problems before they were to happen and then figuring out how to solve these problems. This talent stays with me to this day. It comes in very handy with my work. The problem is that in my personal life, not everyone wants my input – even if it's given with the best of intentions in the nicest way possible.

Someone I know, who was a regular at Al Anon meetings, mentioned an Al Anon comment that I was sure was sarcasm when I first heard it. I learned later that it wasn't – it was pure Al Anon philosophy. That comment was *"Don't rob someone of the dignity of making their own mistakes."* Coming from that child of alcoholic caretaker personality, I don't want anyone to ever have to *endure* a mistake. This was mainly because of my upbringing, making mistakes was intolerable to me, and I assumed it was intolerable for you as well. I know now that it's okay if people – myself especially – make mistakes.

Today, I work on trying my best (and fail at it miserably sometimes) to keep my mouth shut unless asked for input. This can be *really* hard at times.

Intellectualism and Cynicism

Tying back to the terminal uniqueness, both intellectualism and cynicism rely on intelligence – or rather my own aggrandized opinion of my intelligence. Many of us have solved a lot of our problems with brainpower and find it hard to believe we can't do the same thing with this disease. We have tried over and over throughout our lives, but to no avail. As I said earlier: *"If you could have beaten this yourself, you'd have done it by now."*

Cynicism and sarcasm are more arrows in my disease's quiver. If it can convince me that what you're saying about the disease and recovery is stupid, then it has accomplished its mission for another day – and I stay <u>out</u> of recovery.

I like to say that I have the trifecta of cynicism: I'm an alcoholic comedian from New York. With those things working, you really can't get much more of a cynical combination than that. This is another way my disease works against me. If I let the disease get in through *that* side door, I'll be the cleverest, most cynical, sarcastic, intelligent, witty 600-pound guy in the room.

In my past life, when I didn't understand something, there was a part of me that felt threatened. When I felt threatened, I chose to deride it and minimize it through cynical sarcasm. Here's a perfect example: for years, I poo-pooed the concept of positive affirmations. You're telling me that I'm going to conquer my low self-esteem and self-loathing by looking in the mirror and reciting "You're a good person, gosh darn it, and people like you!" *Puh-leeze!*

Yet I never considered the converse. I totally believed all of the <u>negative</u> affirmations I said to myself constantly! These long held self-damning beliefs were most probably installed by my family of origin – and taken as facts by me. If I made a simple mistake or showed any human foible, I was *stupid*. I became aware of this a few years before my mother passed away when she dropped something and said out loud "you stupid so and so!" Ahh, I thought to myself, that's where I got this. So, take a lifetime of dropping things and making mistakes – in other words *being human* – and I had a whole lifetime of negative affirmations about myself. I have, by the way, come to believe that positive affirmations do help change one's beliefs. If you've had a lifetime of negative self-talk, how else will that change except with some "counter-programming?"

Perfectionism

Another critical part of my immature thinking came through perfectionism. As was said earlier, perfectionism is the evil stepsister to compulsive eating. When I was newer in program, I so desperately wanted to find a way to equate my compulsive eating with my alcoholism. After all, I had gotten my alcoholism under control via perfect adherence to sobriety, why couldn't I use those methods for the food?

The problem was simple: I could wish all day for the food and the alcohol to be the same, *but they just weren't.* When I tried to find a way to make them alike, it was through having incredibly rigid lines around the food plan and food choices that were setups for failure. When I then couldn't be perfect, my disease saw it as a way in. *"You're not perfect anymore, so what the heck, you might as well get your due."*

The fact was that I was employing black and white thinking, which in many ways is the product of an immature mind. The world isn't black and white. It is made up of many colors, as well as infinite shades of gray. I needed to come to terms with that.

The trouble for me came from the fact that I was a latchkey kid being raised by similarly immature parents. As a result, I had nobody to teach me the adult concept of life being gray. I was 13 and raising myself, for all intents and purposes. Our society doesn't allow 13 year olds to be parents to other children. Obviously, there are many reasons why, but one of them is because they don't have the maturity to properly parent a child. So my "parent" at 13 years old (myself), taught me the only thing it understood – black and white. Either I was perfect or I was garbage. This, in turn, propagated itself into my relationship with food as I tried to find a path to recovery.

I still had to recognize I had a disease – and I did need to have some "lines in the sand" concerning _some_ foods, but I needed a food plan that I could adhere to *for the long term.* When I was a member of a food program with a very rigid food structure, I saw the same thing: people in a never-ending cycle of abstinence and slipping. The trouble was that this cycle prevented them from working the Steps and moving past the food to deal with the *actual* problems that were driving their addiction. Remember, the food isn't really the problem for most compulsive eaters – it's the solution (albeit a bad one).

Fear of Success/Fear of Unknown Repercussions

Psychologists have discovered that people will choose what is familiar over what is good for them every time. For example, battered women often end up with batterers over and over. They're not consciously choosing them, but there's something familiar about those types of men – a familiarity that the women find oddly reassuring.

At the bottom of some of the fear of success in the food and weight arena is the minefield concerning body image, sexuality, potential relationships, etc. This is a huge thing for many compulsive eaters, especially female compulsive eaters. Since it is such a large subject, I will devote a whole chapter to it later in the book.

The bottom line on "fear of the unknown" still resides with *faith*. There has to be some faith that the program and your Higher Power wouldn't take you this far to drop you on the ground. Yes, there is a new (and possibly scary) world ahead, but the truth is that you have – and will be given – the resources to handle them. As a friend says, "If you're making a commitment to abstinence and recovery, you need to strap in and allow it to take you wherever it leads."

6th Step – Summing Up

The overall view of the 6th Step has to do with two things. Firstly, it involves our being *entirely* ready to have them removed. This could be understood as a theoretical proposition, as in saying "Okay, I'm ready. Now what?" However, the test of whether or not you are truly ready lies in *taking action*. This involves us making our best effort to *change* those negative and ultimately self-destructive behaviors.

This brings us to the second part of this, which is recognizing our humanness and what we're really looking for at this juncture. This work is not going to yield an overnight transformation but rather needs to be seen as a *process*. It's also a *life-long* process, full of many instances of "two steps forward, one step back" (and sometimes the other way around). As it says in the A.A. 12 & 12: *"This does not mean that we expect all our character defects to be lifted out of us as the drive to drink was. A few of them may be, but with most of them we shall have to be content with patient improvement."*

Step 7 – Asking for Help

Step 7: "Humbly asked Him to remove our shortcomings."

In the 7th Step, we hear of humility, through the word "humbly." When I first came to program, I thought of humility in the same sense as that of humiliation. Later, I began to think that the act of humility involved acting like a monk, or Gandhi, or some other pious and devout person. A sponsor disabused me of this thought.

"Humility simply means having an objective view of your place in the world," he said to me. *"You're neither at the top, nor at the bottom. You're just another bozo on the bus."*

I decided I liked his definition of humility. For one thing, it removed all of the grandiosity I had built up around my idea of my place in the world. I vacillated between having a high ego and when that bubble burst, it revealed my true low self-esteem. As I heard it said: *"I was the piece of shit the world revolved around."*

Through studying this Step, I also realized it was, in many ways, out of my hands. There were certain exercises I could do that would help, but the actual "defects" would be removed when it was time for them to go. It was simply up to me to desire them to be removed and do what I could in the real world to help that process.

One of things I started doing when reviewing my day (we'll talk more about that in the Chapter about the 10th Step), was to look at the various things I had not done well, and ask myself, *"How would someone with more recovery have handled the same situation?"* In a way, it's not different from the kind of things pro golfers do: they "visualize" the shot they want to hit. In my case, I tried to "visualize" how I would handle the situation again, if it arose. While this didn't work every time, it did start to creep its way into my consciousness. Slowly, my way of dealing with people – especially conflict – changed.

The one thing about trying to live a program way of life is that it occasionally means you have to make choices that aren't as convenient or easy as other options available to you. The important thing to remember is that the one thing you cannot put a price on is being able to look at yourself in the mirror in the morning and like what you see. As they say: *"The way to get good self-esteem is to do esteemable acts."* In many ways, what is more important than just *liking* yourself is *respecting* yourself. Living a program way of life leads to just that – respecting yourself.

In a program reading called "Just for Today," it says *"Just for Today, I will do someone a good turn and not get found out – if anybody knows of it, it will not count."* Why is it important to not get found out? Because then you know you're doing a good thing for good reasons. If you get in a habit of doing this, you'll be surprised how good you feel. Try it.

The other thing about humility that was so important for me to understand was that I was human. As a friend who leads Big Book workshops says: *"No matter how much I memorize the first 164 pages of the Big Book, the 12 & 12, and everything the program teaches... I don't rise above the level of human being."*

This was something I really needed to internalize. I want to be a better human being, but the fact is that I'm going to slip and fall flat on my face from time to time. I'm going to lose my temper, do something impetuous and stupid – you name it. In the past, I would have flogged myself mercilessly after the fact. Now, I try to acknowledge that I messed up, but try to learn from my mistakes and move on. I'm learning to use "daddy love" on myself. I am neither trying to gloss over what happened with some justification ("after all, I'm human"), nor am I grabbing the stick with which to beat myself.

One of my worst character traits in early sobriety was that I was terribly judgmental of people. What I came to see later was that I had gotten this from my family of origin and that the primary person with whom I was judgmental was me. Once I was able to see myself as human, it became a lot easier to forgive others for being human as well.

The paragraph in the Big Book on acceptance (page 417) speaks of accepting life as it is. To me, the paragraph that immediately follows it is just as vital. It talks about my being critical in this way: *"When I criticize me or you, I am criticizing God's handiwork. I'm saying I know better than God."*

For years, I spoke about this at meetings and retreats, but only really about the part that talked about judging _you_. But that's not what it says. It says *"me or you."* When I am criticizing myself, I'm criticizing God's handiwork. That paragraph also brings into focus how we need to see people – not just life – as neither black nor white, but as gray. It says: *"There is a bit of good in the worst of us and a bit of bad in the best of us."*

Being less judgmental also helps in meetings. It's very easy to go to a lot of meetings and after a while, it's like being part of a large family. The problem with large families is that the various members can get on your nerves after a while. We cannot afford this. These are our fellow members and I never know when one of them might just play a critical role in my continued recovery. As I said earlier: don't shoot the people in your own foxhole. One of my favorite sayings is: *"Be nice to your sponsees, you never know when one of them might become your sponsor."*

Chapter 9 – Steps 8 & 9: Facing your Past

Step 8: "Made a list of all persons we had harmed, and became willing to make amends to them all."

Having taken some time to review and work on your character defects, the time comes for what can be the toughest part of the Steps: facing – *literally* – your past. In my case, it required me to pull out my 4th Step and start making the amends list based on what I had written earlier. At the same time, I found myself thinking of more and more people to whom amends needed to be made.

This Step, more than any other Step, is one that requires a person to work in close coordination with a sponsor. On my first 8th Step list, I was ready to put down everyone and everything I ever wronged, thought badly of, or even those about whom I had impure thoughts. Everything was going to go into that dumpster. I'm sure in my zeal I probably considered adding to that list some ant I stepped on in the first grade. This was where my sponsor was immensely helpful.

I vacillated from self-flagellation over every little thing I had ever done in my life to wanting to gloss over huge things out of some buried fear of having to deal with them. I often wanted to wheel out the old "except when to do so would injure them or others" loophole. I had even tried to make a case that just dredging up this nasty little past and presenting it to them will make *them* feel bad. So maybe I shouldn't do it, right? This reasoning got my sponsor smiling knowingly, but shaking his head. No sale.

Another excuse I had with one particularly nasty amend I had to make concerned a situation where I was wronged by the other person about ten times more than I had wronged him. My apologizing for my part, I reasoned, would simply reinforce to that person that he was right and I knew he wasn't! Isn't it wrong to falsely make a person feel that they were right when they weren't?

My sponsor's reply was annoying, but also spot on, as I later realized. "Well then that's something he should put on <u>his</u> 8th Step list – but we're dealing with <u>your</u> 8th Step list, John."

Another controversy among those who work with the Steps concerns the idea of putting yourself on the amends list. Those who follow a strict A.A. background will say you shouldn't. However, I truly believe the majority of compulsive eaters *should* put themselves on the list. In this addiction, more than many others, the major recipient of the damage from our disease was ourselves.

For me, I looked at how my food obsession and my eating had turned what could have been a large, wonderful life into a small, isolated one. It led to a lack of intimate relationships and a stunted growth – and many wasted years.

Moreover, I was a brutal and unforgiving taskmaster and perfectionist – mostly to myself. I treated myself much worse than I ever treated anyone else. Today, I take to heart something I heard at an Al Anon meeting once: "Never talk to yourself any worse than you'd talk to a child you love and care about."

Finally, if a Step 8 list is slow to come, remember what I said earlier: the Steps should flow easily. If you feel stuck, look back on some of the previous Steps and ask yourself if more work needs to be done there.

Step 9: Facing Your Past

Step 9: "Made direct amends to such people wherever possible, except when to do so would injure them or others."

In my opinion, the Ninth Step is the hardest one, because it requires us to put ourselves on the line. Up until now, most of what we've done with the Steps has been pure lip and pen work. Now we have to take action. As my sponsor reminded me again, "the chapter is called 'Into Action', not 'Into Thinking',"

This is also another case of the process being "front loaded with pain." What this means is that there is a lot of fear and trepidation when starting the process, but as you go along the amends get easier to do because many amends go well, and it reinforces in us that we are doing the right thing. Our self-esteem grows by knowing we are doing something tough that will make us better human beings. There's no better feeling than knowing you've gone through a day being the best person you could be – no guilt, no regrets.

One of my first memories of the amends process in action happened when I was newly sober. A friend named Stan, who had gotten sober about the same time as I had, was wrestling with a major amends he needed to make. He had been a house painter and had worked with (and for) his best friend. Then one day, right before he got sober, he quit on his friend with no notice, leaving him terribly in the lurch. His actions had hurt a friend and ruined their friendship. He spoke about it at meetings quite a bit because it was eating at him terribly. He kept saying that he really needed to make those amends.

One day, Stan came waltzing into the meeting whistling and obviously in a great mood. "Well," he said with a smile, "I finally made that amends today!"

"I guess it went pretty well," I replied, noting his demeanor.

"On the contrary," he said. "The guy told me to screw off and slammed the phone down in my ear."

"Then why are you so happy?" I asked.

Stan smiled. "Because it's _his_ problem now," he replied.

He was right. He had reached out in an honest effort to clean up his side of the street. The fact that his efforts were rebuffed was something outside of his control. He had done all he could do. From that day on, the burden of guilt about that incident was removed from him.

Making a sincere amends is not a "get out of hell free" card. The key thing, as I have been taught, is that it's called "amends," not "apologies." The difference between the two has to do with the fact that in addition to the apology, we are expected to _amend_ our behavior – to change it going forward. It's of little consequence if we apologize for a bad behavior, and then keep repeating that same behavior in the future. Amends for continued bad behavior aren't amends at all, they are just ways of trying to make us feel better about whatever bad behavior we continue to do.

If we are going to change our lives, it must start with our actions. We are human, so we may stumble and take a few steps backwards, but we attempt to move forward and make ourselves into better people.

There are different ways to prioritize the amends to be made. Some people try to get the toughest ones out of the way first, while others want to get a bunch of the "smaller" ones done first.

Another technique some people do is to put the amends in three categories:

1. Amends I'm willing to make
2. Amends I'm not ready to make right now.
3. Amends I will never make.

For sponsees that need to do amends in this way, I tell them that it's fine, just be willing to be open to a possible change down the road. What I've found is that the amends process sometimes begins to take on a momentum of its own. Once the person begins to see and feel the benefits of making amends, he or she is often willing to start moving the amends from one category to another.

As to the amends themselves, many of them will be received well. People often like being magnanimous, and accepting a well-made amends makes everyone feel good. One of the things I remind my sponsees is that the amends should be straightforward and simple. Telling people _why_ you are making the amends sometimes subverts the amends themselves. Saying, "I'm in a 12 Step program and I _have_ to make amends" makes the person think the amends are somehow a selfish action. "So if you weren't in a 12 Step program," they might think to themselves, "you probably wouldn't even consider making these amends." My advice: just make the amends and keep the motive to yourself.

What about those tougher amends? There are amends where the other person might have done just as much – if not more – harm to you. The words of my sponsor come to mind "remember, this is your 9th Step, not his." If I have worked the previous steps well, I can do this with an open heart and accept whatever comes back. Sometimes they will be well received, but often – at least in terms of these "tough" amends – they might not be taken well. Often these "tough" amends are with someone where there might have been terrible animosity in the past. We need to be examples of recovery and even if we feel their point of view is 100% wrong – we simply listen. I always love the response I was taught in Al Anon: "you might be right." The unspoken second part of this sentence is "on the other hand, you might very well be full of shit." The last thing we want to do is to respond emotionally to his views and end up creating even *more* wreckage. Then that wreckage will require amends – and you could end up in an infinite amends loop!

The other hard part about these amends is the inevitable desire to stand there after these amends have been made waiting for the other person's amends to come back to you. The fact is that while this may happen sometimes, often it will not – and as with all expectations, that will lead to disappointment and frustration. If you don't feel you can do an amends without simmering animosity and a desire for reciprocation – wait on that particular amends until you feel you can do so without *any* rancor or expectations towards that person.

So how does one make the amends – and in what form? I've always been taught that amends should always be made in person – eye to eye – unless it is impossible to do so. If a person is not within driving distance, it might be someone to put on your "later" list in the hope that you might at some point travel to their location (or they might be in your area). In decreasing order of acceptability after face-to-face would be over the phone, a mailed letter, or only in the last resort, an email.

Then there are the cases where the person has passed on. For me, and for others, the best we could do was to go to the gravesite and speak our peace. I realize that a gravesite visit isn't really necessary, but often it makes a symbolic impact to do it this way. As to amends to the deceased person, obviously we cannot make direct amends. However, if it is a financial amends, perhaps they can be made to a child or other relative of the person. Other times perhaps a donation to a charity that person might have supported or one with some symbolic significance.

As to other types of amends, I've known of people who have done what they could to "pass it on," Some people will volunteer at some social service activity, in lieu of the amends they can never make. The idea here is to feel like you've done your best to "clean the slate,"

The most important part of this goes back to the idea that you have to be willing to go to any lengths in this amends and recovery process. This is about cleaning up our side of the street, no matter what the repercussions.

My favorite story along these lines comes from a woman who is an old timer in the Los Angeles area. She had been, along with her overeating, a shoplifter during her eating career. She decided the only way she would be able to conquer the eating disease was to clean the slate concerning the shoplifting. With that in mind, she decided she needed to go to the main department store from which she had shoplifted and ask how she might make amends. She left a note for her husband on the kitchen table that said, "If I am not home when you read this, I'm probably in jail."

This was how determined she was to do the right thing. She showed up at the department store and explained her situation, which baffled the sales clerk. She called for her manager who said, "Well, we've had this type of thing before, but usually in the form of a letter with a check enclosed. We've never had someone show up." In the end, they decided the best thing this old timer could do was to make a contribution to a charity of her choice, in the amount she felt was equal to the amount she had stolen. She did just that, and has been in program for over _50_ years as of this writing.

Chapter 10 – Steps 10 & 11: Moving toward the program ideal

Step 10: "Continued to take personal inventory, and when we were wrong, promptly admitted it."

For many of us, the 9th Step is a lifelong process and as such we can – at some point – say, "okay, time to move on to the next Steps." For most people, it's impossible to do all of one's amends in a timely manner. Some people will be hard to track down, others will be on our "not yet" list. Does that mean we screech to a halt in our work on the Steps because we haven't totally finished our 9th Step? I think not.

Various people have divided the Steps into groups. I heard early in my recovery that the first three Steps were "the give up Steps." Steps 4 through 9 were the "clean up Steps", and Steps 10, 11, and 12 were the "keep up Steps."

When I think about my personal history and my introduction to the 12 Steps, I think the first Step that I actually "got" at a core level was the 10th Step. In my family of origin, admitting you were wrong about anything made you a target. For many years, even when I was wrong about things, I would work desperately through incredible mental gymnastics and pretzel logic to defend my (erroneous) position – trying to justify and rationalize it. It took a lot of energy, and in the end was usually fruitless.

What a relief the 10th Step was to me. Now, I could simply stop and assess the situation and if I was wrong I could stop dead in my tracks and say simply: "I'm sorry, I screwed up." I didn't have to valiantly try to defend my position, and I didn't have to get angry if someone pointed out I was wrong. A long time ago – when I was newly sober – I heard a great old-timer say this about being angry during an argument: *"If you're right, you have no need to be angry. If you're wrong, you have no right to be angry."*

As a result of this early lesson, it was the Step I did earliest and the best – and I still do. I just wish I didn't have to do it so much. My biggest problem – and one of the areas I need the most work on is – as the A.A. 12 & 12 says: *"Restraint of pen and tongue."*

I have amended this to read *"Restraint of pen and tongue and 'send' button."*

The longer you're in program, the easier it is to come to terms with messing up – and the quicker you are to recognize it. As part of all of my work in the earlier Steps, I came to the realization that as a human being I am going to screw up from time to time. My job is to learn from each of these incidents so as to try to not repeat them in the future – or to at least lessen the intensity of my failings and mitigate the damage they might cause.

One of the things that I have observed in myself is the physical <u>need</u> sometimes to *"blow off steam"* at someone or something. Once I realized this was something I could not totally conquer by program aphorisms or self-talk, I began to try to tackle the need to relieve the pressure in a different way. I realized I could re-direct that "steam" in another direction.

What I have learned to do is something I read about in a biography of U.S. President Harry Truman. One can imagine that the office of President of the United States comes with about as much frustration as any job in the world. Not being a dictator, Harry Truman had to work with Congress, deal with an often hostile press, as well as many people not keen on seeing him succeed. As a result, the stress on him (as with all Presidents) was enormous.

Truman's way to "blow off steam" was to sit down and write excoriating letters to many of the people causing him grief. He would vent vociferously and often with more than a smattering of four letter words. When he was done writing these letters, he would neatly fold them and put them in his desk drawer. It was the act of *writing* these letters – to be able to "speak his mind" – that helped him "blow off" that steam. The story (as I read it) was that when he left office and his desk was shipped off to his new Presidential Library in Independence, Missouri – the curators there found these letters – four letter words and all. I recently read a book that was published containing many of these letters.

The point here is that there is a lot to be said for allowing yourself to "blow off steam," while at the same time not doing so directly until "cooler heads have prevailed." I will often write a reply to some particularly snarky email sent to me – often in the same tone as the original letter. The difference between the old me and the new me is that I save it as a draft and come back later or the next day. If I still feel that way with a cooler head, then off it goes. Otherwise, the delete button works just fine. Most often, the email gets an edit, making it less emotional. Often finding a way to say things with less confrontation can do more toward getting a person their desired results. As they say in Al Anon: *"say what you mean, mean what you say – just don't say it mean."*

With both this Step and the next, the Big Book is quite specific on what we need to do:

"When we retire at night, we constructively review our day. Were we resentful, selfish, dishonest or afraid? Do we owe an apology? Have we kept something to ourselves which should be discussed with another person at once? Were we kind and loving toward all? What could we have done better? Were we thinking of ourselves most of the time? Or were we thinking of what we could do for others, of what we could pack into the stream of life?"

Before you pick up the whip to begin flailing away at yourself after reading the above paragraph, remember that these are *ideals* towards which we are aiming – not actions and attitudes that are easily achieved. The key here is to be heading down the road towards the type of person who might at some point achieve these lofty goals – if only *for today*. Just like abstinence – it might be followed by another day, and then another. If you are like me, those days are rarely consecutive for a long period.

In the next section, the Big Book brings things down to Earth:

"But we must be careful not to drift into worry, remorse or morbid reflection, for that would diminish our usefulness to others. After making our review we ask God's forgiveness and inquire what corrective measures should be taken."

The longer you are around and working a program, the less you find yourself willing to wait until the end of the day to assess where you might have been wrong during the day. I believe that I have gained "that annoying little guy" that whispers in my ear whenever I've done something wrong. I get this feeling in the pit of my stomach that tells me "there's a disturbance in the force," and that I need to make things right. When that happens, I might as well listen to that little guy, because he won't leave me alone until I do. The fact is that I feel so much better after making the amends – and that's what counts.

Step 11 – Adjusting our will to reality

Step 11: "Sought through prayer and meditation to improve our conscious contact with God as we understood Him, praying only for knowledge of His will for us and the power to carry that out."

When I first came into the program, the idea of "prayer and meditation" seemed daunting. Was I to become a monk, deeply immersed in this practice? My sponsor disabused me of the notion, saying "prayer is talking to God, and meditation is listening for a reply." Another person told me to think of meditation as merely *focused thought*. Those two concepts were good enough for me.

The Big Book has some specific advice on this practice, and it comes immediately after the direction on finishing your day.

"On awakening let us think about the twenty-four hours ahead. We consider our plans for the day. Before we begin, we ask God to direct our thinking, especially asking that it be divorced from self-pity, dishonest or self-seeking motives. Under these conditions we can employ our mental faculties with assurance, for after all God gave us brains to use. Our thought-life will be placed on a much higher plane when our thinking is cleared of wrong motives.

In thinking about our day we may face indecision. We may not be able to determine which course to take. Here we ask God for inspiration, an intuitive thought or a decision. We relax and take it easy. We don't struggle. We are often surprised how the right answers come after we have tried this for a while. What used to be the hunch or the occasional inspiration gradually becomes a working part of the mind. Being still inexperienced and having just made conscious contact with God, it is not probable that we are going to be inspired at all times. We might pay for this presumption in all sorts of absurd actions and ideas. Nevertheless, we find that our thinking will, as time passes, be more and more on the plane of inspiration. We come to rely upon it.

We usually conclude the period of meditation with a prayer that we be shown all through the day what our next step is to be, that we be given whatever we need to take care of such problems. We ask especially for freedom from self-will, and are careful to make no request for ourselves only. We may ask for ourselves, however, if others will be helped. We are careful never to pray for our own selfish ends. Many of us have wasted a lot of time doing that and it doesn't work. You can easily see why.

If circumstances warrant, we ask our wives or friends to join us in morning meditation. If we belong to a religious denomination which requires a definite morning devotion, we attend to that also. If not members of religious bodies, we sometimes select and memorize a few set prayers which emphasize the principles we have been discussing. There are many helpful books also. Suggestions about these may be obtained from one's priest, minister, or rabbi. Be quick to see where religious people are right. Make use of what they offer.

As we go through the day we pause, when agitated or doubtful, and ask for the right thought or action. We constantly remind ourselves we are no longer running the show, humbly saying to ourselves many times each day "Thy will be done." We are then in much less danger of excitement, fear, anger, worry, self-pity, or foolish decisions. We become much more efficient. We do not tire so easily, for we are not burning up energy foolishly as we did when we were trying to arrange life to suit ourselves.

It works – it really does."

From my experience, when I start my day doing the above action, or some version of it, my day is invariably better than if I do not. I am setting a foundation for myself for the day. I am stopping to reflect on the day ahead and how I am going to tackle it. I'm taking some time to try to get in a 12 Step "head space" so that I can try to align myself with the program precepts I have been taught.

Then there are those _other_ days. Occasionally something happens to jar me out of my routine and I have to "hit the ground running." When I do this and I don't get my usual time to center myself before proceeding, it's like I have been thrown out of a speeding car – all I'm trying to do is keep myself from going face down in the gravel.

It's important to keep in mind that the Big Book was first published in 1939, when A.A. was newly derivative of the Christian Oxford Group. Since then, Twelve Step organizations have evolved to the point where it would be impossible to dictate any exact way of "prayer and meditation." What of the atheist? Does he or she pray "to whom it may concern"?

It's perfectly fine – if you are so inclined – to start with some formal type of prayer and meditation. There are volumes written on this – both in formal religious texts as well as many "how to" books (mostly on meditation).

Let me address those for whom prayer and meditation might be a foreign concept. Even if you do not want to try anything like formal prayer and meditation (but you might want to keep an open mind about trying it sometime in the future), there are some things you might consider as alternatives. The idea of starting your day with a reminder of what kind of life you're trying to lead is helpful. As has been said, "Be the author of your day, not the victim of the events." Or, I heard in another 12 Step meeting once: "Act, don't _re_act."

How exactly do you start on such a road? Here's a thought: when you get up in the morning, don't turn on the TV or the computer. Have a cup of coffee and look out the window. While early morning meditation had always been difficult for me, a number of years ago I got something that helped immensely: a dog. Every morning, I take my coffee and walk through the neighborhood while Laila sniffs every tree and chases every squirrel. During that time, I think about the day ahead and what I'm going to have to do to maintain an even keel and stay serene.

I also try to think about things that I have been struggling with and how to handle them better. There is a little voice inside me that I personally think of as my Higher Power. I try desperately to listen and to be willing to keep an open mind about what that voice might be saying. Often that little voice collides with my desires and my will. If I can truly stay open and quiet, sometimes that voice cuts through the noise in my head and becomes clear. The reality is that often I don't like what that voice is saying, but I know that it's usually right and I should listen to it.

I am often asked at retreats "How do I know what is God's will and what is my will?" Certainly there are libraries full of books written by men and women much more knowledgeable on the subject than I, and the consensus seems to be "darned if we know." Nonetheless, I have found that little voice is telling me what I need to hear; I just have to be willing to get still and listen to it.

As to prayer, I avoid praying for specific things – both for myself and for others. Why? I think for me to be deciding what's best for me and then praying for it is the height of ego and arrogance. That certainly goes double as to me praying for what I think is best for *you*.

I will hear someone say at a meeting "I'm up for this job, please pray that I get it." What if that job is the job from hell and that person will be miserable there? Meanwhile, their dream job might have been the next one they would have found had they not gotten the one for which they were praying? In that case, I would have prayed for the *worst* thing for them.

Some of the biggest disappointments I've had in life – when I look back at them – were exactly what I needed. As the program slogan says, "Rejection is sometimes God's protection." In some cases, I was praying for a bicycle and God had given me a Lexus (which I didn't see because I was too busy looking for the bicycle). If I have one concrete belief, it's that everything is happening the way it's supposed to – my job is to go along for the ride and accept it.

One of my favorite quotes came from the late Steve Jobs: *"You can't connect the dots looking forward; you can only connect them looking backward. So you have to trust that the dots will somehow connect in your future. You have to trust in something — your gut, destiny, life, karma, whatever. This approach has never let me down, and it has made all the difference in my life."*

Thus, when I pray for anything for others, it's simply to hope they get what is best for them.

I think the most important word in the Steps is the word "*only*" in the 11th Step. I'm supposed to pray *only* for the ability to accept the way things are supposed to be. Previously, my concept of a God was one that gave me all of the things on my wish list and did as I told him. That's not God – *that's Santa Claus.*

Nowadays, I strive to be happy with what I have. I look to what the Big Book says:

"We are taught to differentiate between our wants (which are never satisfied) and our needs (which are always provided for)." – Alcoholics Anonymous, p. 560

I know if left to my own devices, my wants would be limitless. When I was newly sober, I heard a story that made me rethink my whole idea of happiness and contentment. I got sober in Fairfield County, Connecticut. A friend of mine who was in A.A. grew up in my hometown of Greenwich, the son of very wealthy parents. He said that he remembered being a young child and hearing his mother complaining to his father because the neighbors had just gotten a second Rolls-Royce while they had only one. "I was only a young child," he said. "But I knew even then that anyone who needed a second Rolls-Royce to be happy would never be happy."

How often had I thought "If only I had... <fill in the blank>... I'd be happy"? If truth be told, if I did get whatever it was I was hoping for, I *would* be happy – for a millisecond. Soon after that, I would move the goalposts and find something else I needed to be happy. It would never end.

I am so far from where I was when I came into program. Then, I was rabidly atheist. I had my brain on a pedestal. Man was the highest of existence, and since I was in the top one percentile of intelligence, I was on top. I was *so* on top that I couldn't stop drinking and eating and I was ready to kill myself. Looking back, I should have donated my ego to science for study.

Today, I understand that I'm not on top of humanity. In addition, I realize humans aren't king of the hill either. I often pick up the paper and read about people being eaten by sharks. This should be a powerful humility lesson for all of us. We're not even at the top of the food chain! We compulsive overeaters could be compulsively overeaten!

One of the first retreats I led was in Portland, Oregon. I flew in early and took a drive up to Mount St. Helens. As you drive along the road, for as far as you can see, there are trees that were blown over in the initial blast from that volcano. You drive for quite a while before reaching the visitor center – all the way there looking at hundreds, possibly thousands of once tall trees lying on their sides. Once you see this, you get a better idea that we are all just ants on this big blue ball.

The other thing that was very off-putting to me when I came to program was the memorized prayers. The Lord's Prayer, in particular, stuck in my craw. I complained to my sponsor that "this is a Christian prayer, we shouldn't be saying it." He asked me where exactly the reference to Christ was. He then suggested we sit down and go over the prayer word by word so that I could show him which words were offensive to me. I sputtered "No... it's not any one word, it's the concept!" He smiled at me and replied,

"John... we're not saying a concept, we're saying words." From that day forward, I stopped arguing about prayers at meetings. For me one of the most important passages in any writing is "forgive us our trespasses, as we forgive those who trespass against us." In other words, if I want forgiveness for my screw-ups, then I better start doing some forgiving of others.

My final words about a Higher Power come from an anonymous quote I heard from a program friend: *"Don't tell your God how big your problems are – tell your problems how big your God is."*

Chapter 11 – Step 12: Trust God and Work with Another

Step 12, Part 1: Having had a spiritual awakening as the result of these steps, we tried to carry this message to compulsive overeaters

---

This is another example of a two-part Step, this more than any other. If you have a sentence with two totally disparate clauses, then they should be made into two sentences. The same is true with Steps. And the 12ᵗʰ Step, more than any other, contains two ideas that do not relate to each other. To a lot of people and cultures, 13 is an unlucky number – so the 13 Steps were out. A case could even be made that the 12 Step is *three* Steps, with the first part concerning a spiritual awakening, the second about carrying the message and the third about practicing these principles in all our affairs. For today, however, let's take the two parts of the 12ᵗʰ Step one at a time.

Having had a spiritual awakening as the result of these steps, we tried to carry this message to compulsive overeaters...

This part of the 12ᵗʰ Step has the most misread word of all of the 12 Steps. Read the Step carefully: "Having had a spiritual awakening as *the* result of these Steps," not "as *a* result of these Steps." While to some this may seem nitpicky, there is a major difference in the two readings. The result of the Steps is *one* thing: a spiritual awakening from which all else flows. Besides removing the desire to engage in inappropriate food behaviors, many character defects – mainly, our obsession with ourselves and our immaturity – are also removed. This is no small feat! There are many benefits to this spiritual awakening – and I will talk more in depth about them in the chapter "The Final Gift."

Service

I had a friend who had been in "Smokers Anonymous" many years ago – it has since changed its name to "Nicotine Anonymous." One of the problems, he had noted, was that most of the meetings were pretty small and were mostly populated by people <u>trying</u> to stop smoking. There were very few long-term members. This was not, he had surmised from talking to fellow members, because the program didn't work – the problem was in many ways it worked *too* well. After a certain amount of time without smoking, people felt they no longer needed the program and drifted away. Obviously they had gotten a good handle on the first step – at least enough that they might very well not smoke again. They stopped working the steps past that. They never got out of themselves to realize that since they were given this gift, they needed to be willing to help pass this gift on to others. They never advanced in their recovery to think about someone other than themselves. The result was there were very few sponsors in that program. It was more "quitting with group support" than working a 12 Step program.

Imagine if this was the case with our food programs. As it is, finding sponsors is not always easy. Imagine however, that not only was it hard to find sponsors, but also people to do many of the other service positions. In this respect, I'm not only talking about at a group level, but above group level. Imagine if the first time you had decided to go to a meeting that the people who make your local meeting lists, or websites, or who reply to messages left on answering machines, or intergroup offices – didn't exist. Where would you have found a meeting? It's not like people are standing out on the corner yelling it out to passers-by – or handing out flyers.

If others had not been there to "carry this message to other compulsive eaters," you might never have found any recovery. I remember a number of years ago I attended a meeting where a small group of us continually took the service positions – not because we wanted to – but because nobody else would volunteer to do so. This was not a small meeting, but one that had a reasonably robust attendance. It was a Sunday morning meeting and I think a lot of the people didn't want to be "tied down" to a six-month service commitment – even if it was a shared commitment. As it was, many of the members would attend one week, but not the next. We had a lot of "part time" attendees.

Finally, the "inner group" of us that constantly swapped positions decided it was time for "rotation of service" and chose to not raise our hands at election time. The result was that nobody else raised their hands – and though it pained us to do so – we let the meeting close. I always wanted to stand outside that door on the Sunday mornings after the meeting closed to see the people who attended part time show up and find the door locked. Then I would say to them "the meeting is closed because _you_ didn't pitch in to help it survive." It was not a desire to give an "I told you so," but rather to point out that all 12 Step programs are not manned by a staff of professionals, they are manned by _us_.

I learned very early in my first program that the key to recovery was "trust God, clean house, and help another person." Whenever I am having problems, getting out of my self-centered world is the key to relief. This is true even if it is just to make a phone call – and instead of grousing about my problems – start the conversation with "how are _you_ doing?"

That's why I sponsor. That's why I always have at least one service commitment a week at a meeting, and it's why I require my sponsees to do the same. As soon as they have 30 days, I tell them it's time to quit auditing the program and get involved. I often tell them to start sponsoring that quickly as well. The 12 Step programs of the world are saving lives every day – they certainly saved mine. I need to remember that had I had the unfortunate luck to be born 100 years ago, I'd almost assuredly be dead by now. The reason? No program would have existed to give me a _chance_ at recovery. Since this gift is available to us, it is incumbent on all of us to not only keep it going, but to help it thrive. All of our service is money in the bank. Right now we may be making a deposit, but you never know when you might need to make a withdrawal.

A while back, there was a movie called "Pay It Forward," The plot of the story was about a kid who had an idea to do good things for people – without expecting anything in return. When the person he helped asks how he or she might repay the debt, they are told to "pay it forward" – in other words they should go do a good deed for someone else. When I saw the movie, I remember thinking "this isn't a new concept, this is what we in 12 Step groups do every day!" When I was newly sober, I didn't have a car and people drove me to meetings constantly – and took me home. Today, whenever I can, I repay the favor by driving people to and from meetings.

When I think about some of my home meetings here in L.A., often a lot of the same people are doing the service. At the same time, I realize that this group of people is mainly made up of those who have stayed around for 10, 20, and even 30 years. When I think of the people I look up to in program, they have one thing in common: they're all doing the same things today, especially service, – many years into their recovery – they were doing in their first few months. If it ain't broke, don't fix it!

The amazing process of 12 Step programs is how they often "put the cart before the horse." I was pushed into doing service without seeing the value of it at the time. To me, this was just the old-timers getting people to run the meetings for them. The first job they gave me is one that doesn't even exist anymore: cleaning up ashtrays. Then I made coffee, set up chairs and eventually moved on to other service positions. What I see now was the main thing service did for me was that it got me out of myself. In retrospect, I can see the benefit of getting out of myself, and later how it translated into trying to be permanently removed from that prison of self. An extra benefit of service is it breaks the isolation that envelops many compulsive eaters when they are new to program. Most service requires you to interact with other members of the program. While this may seem a bit scary if you've been by yourself for a long time, it's one of the first baby steps on the road to recovery.

In terms of moving up to Service Boards above the meeting level, I recommend to my sponsees that they wait until they've done the first eleven Steps. Carrying the message and other 12th Step work at that level comes with a certain assumption that the other Steps have been done. The main reason – and I can vouch for this – is that often this kind of board work in close quarters can bring up all kinds of character defects. This is the reason that many Service Boards have abstinence requirements, often with the codicil that people have worked a Fourth and Fifth Step. You should have done some work on yourself, which will make it easier to be able to work with others.

Sponsorship

In the chapter about Step 2, I talked about sponsorship, but from the perspective of getting one and using one – but what about the experience of *being* one? This is an area in which I think food programs have dropped the ball. Every 12 Step program needs a strong sponsorship "chain" to exist. Yet I will go to meetings with 50 people in attendance, and when available sponsors are asked to identify themselves, only one or two people stand up. A program could spend many thousands of dollars (at the World level) in publicity and getting the word out about itself, but if the new people that publicity might attract come to a meeting and can't find a sponsor, all that money and effort will have gone to waste.

I think there are a couple of reasons for this lack of available sponsors. First and foremost there isn't a culture where sponsors insist that *their* sponsees need to become sponsors (who in turn insist *their* sponsees sponsor, and so on). Perhaps this is done out of an abundance of caution to not be too controlling, but I think a case can be made to sponsees as to why sponsoring will bolster their recovery.

As a sponsor, I like my sponsees to get into sponsoring relatively early in the process. I rarely get much resistance to requests of my sponsees until I say "I'd like you to start sponsoring." Then you almost hear the "beep, beep, beep" as they start trying to back away. "I'm not ready to sponsor," they insist. Read the Big Book – there were people helping others with *days* of sobriety. If you've been abstinent for three days, you can help someone who can't string two days together.

"I won't know what to say. I'm afraid I'll mess people up with bad advice." Well, there's part of the problem right there. Don't give advice: share your experience, strength and hope with your sponsees – nothing more. As I mentioned in the chapter on the 2nd Step, my sponsors have never had any compunction in telling me when they didn't have any experience with a problem I was having – and I admired them for being willing to tell me so. There was no ego there – only a sincere desire to help.

If you have a problem with a sponsee that you cannot figure out, kick it up the chain. Ask your sponsor for help with it. If your sponsor can't help, he'll ask his sponsor, and that sponsor will ask his sponsor and so on. Here in L.A., the end of that chain is often a revered old timer who can answer almost anything, and if she can't she'll call God – and he will take her call.

I cannot tell you how many times I have hung up a phone after talking to a sponsee and said out loud to myself, "Okay... did you hear what you suggested to _him_ to do? Perhaps you might consider doing that yourself!" That is one of the benefits of being a sponsor. The fact is that nobody should be on either end of the sponsor chain. People without a sponsor – no matter how much time they have in program – worry me. There certainly might be reasons why one would be without a sponsor for a limited amount of time, but to be without one for long feels like ego to me. After a certain amount of time in program, you shouldn't be without sponsees either. We're all supposed to be adults here, and not being willing to sponsor is saying "I want to take and take, but not give back." It's a sign of wanting to stay "a child" in program for as long as possible – also not a good sign.

The hardest thing about being a sponsor is finding that fine line concerning control. I find I have to continually "ping" myself to decide if my ego is getting involved in a sponsee relationship. This used to happen to me a lot when I was younger. My control issues didn't get better until I had spent some time reading Al Anon literature. From that education, I "got" that I am merely a guide, not a boss or dictator. I need to learn to not judge, but be there to help and be of service. I did have a right, however, to draw boundaries – especially of my time. I had one sponsee who would tell me of his problems until I told him I had to go. We did this for over a year – until he left program. I had to learn the old adage "carry the message, not the person." I learned from that experience that I needed to stop being an "amateur shrink" and work at being a good 12 Step sponsor. Now I ask questions like "what character defect do you think this problem is bringing up?"

The key to sponsorship – much like a therapist – is objectivity. You and your sponsee are partners in recovery, both yours and your sponsee's recovery. The onus is still on the member, not the sponsor. Again: "_carry the message, not the person._"

Carrying the message to those not yet in program

When I came to my first program, I learned very quickly that 12 Step calls were taken very seriously. When someone reaches out to a 12 Step organization, that first impression can literally be the difference between life and death. What I learned was to keep the discussion exclusively to what had happened to me. The last thing any person with the kind of personality that leads to addiction wants to hear is "here is what _you_ should do."

When I get calls from someone not in program, I explain what the program is and what it is not, how it works and what is – or rather what is _not_ expected of them. I tell them a bit of my story, how the program has helped me lose and maintain a significant amount of weight, and how that weight loss is secondary to the serenity and peace I've found in program. Then I stop talking and listen. Often, for many it's the first person they've talked to about this subject that has wanted to listen rather than to tell them _"what they should do."_

Occasionally, I will have relatives of people come to me to try to get their loved ones help. I will give them a meeting list and my phone number and tell them that if their loved one wants help, I am here and the meetings are here. They often respond with a plea for me to "visit" the person. I know from experience that this won't work. Sometimes in A.A., an old timer will have someone say to them "My husband drinks and he doesn't want to stop!" The response is "well then make him a drink!" The reality is that if someone is 300-plus pounds and happy, it's none of my business. On the other hand, I don't think truly happy people get to be 300-plus pounds. The kind of weight we often see in newcomers to food programs doesn't happen merely because a person likes food – although he or she might tell themselves that falsehood.

I do, however, counsel the people who have come to me about their friend or loved one to consider going to Al Anon, as this person's addiction is obviously bothering _them_. While Al Anon is geared towards families of alcoholics, most families of any type of addict will be able to relate what is said there.

The main reason we need to have a "hands off" attitude when it comes to approaching active addicts is that we must be careful about "polluting the waters." You can end up giving someone a BAD impression of the program by trying to jam it down their throats when they don't want it and when they're not ready. The result could be that due to that bad impression, they might _never_ get it! There was a recent high profile example of a sitcom actor who had two producers who were in a recovery program. They tried an aggressive "hands on" approach to disastrous ends. It not only blew up in their face, but in many ways the resulting bad publicity (most of it caused by the actor) gave that program a black eye that may have turned off many potential members.

It's all about surrender... and people have to be at or near their bottom before they might have the ability to hear the message. Frankly, they may have more eating to do. Unfortunately, it's also a deadly disease and sometimes a person's bottom is just a little below the death line – meaning, they don't make it. It's sad, but also powerful for those of us who see it. After a demoralizing experience with a friend who didn't get the program (and later died), a sponsor told me "Some people are put into your life to be bad examples." He wasn't trying to be funny.

When it comes to this Step, the Big Book, in "Working With Others", is the ultimate guide. It says *"We find it a waste of time to keep chasing a man who cannot or will not work with you."*

Unlike other addictions, some of the sufferers of compulsive eating are very obvious. As Orson Welles once said *"Gluttony is not a secret vice."* When we are in a public place and see someone hundreds of pounds overweight, there is a temptation to want to go up to them and tell them about the relief we have found. Unfortunately, this would almost assuredly rebound, as they would hear any unsolicited comment including any 12 Step program for eaters as being a thinly veiled criticism of their weight.

What I do, if appropriate, is to find some way to simply mention that I used to weigh 100 pounds more than I do now. This is the equivalent of casting a fishing lure into the water. A lot of times I get a nibble. I know when I was battling with my weight, I always had my radar up about people who had lost weight. I was in search of "the magic answer." If the prospect decides to ask about it, I offhandedly mention my food program and what it's done for me – but I'm careful to keep it simple. Then I wait for them to ask me more. If they do, fine – if they don't, at least I've planted a seed. You never know what sprouts up from the seeds you plant.

At the end of the day, recovery isn't for those who want it, or for those who need it – it's for those who do it.

Most importantly, the best way to "carry the message" about your program is to have physical recovery. Being at or moving toward a healthy body weight – as O.A.'s definition of abstinence now says – is probably one of the most important ways to carry the message. Obviously, there is so much more to 12 Step recovery than just weight loss, but the sad fact is that people who might need such a program will judge people touting their membership in that program based on their weight. In L.A., we had to "accept the things we could not change" and try to have only people of a healthy body weight at Health Fairs. Otherwise, the presence of an overweight person there – even if he or she has lost hundreds of pounds already – would be counter-productive. We don't like this, but living the Serenity Prayer means having to accept peoples' prejudices as "things we cannot change" and having healthy body weight people as representatives at those public events as being "things we can change." Perhaps someday societal perceptions about eating disorders will change, but for now, this is how it is.

Practicing These Principles

Step 12, Part Deux: To Practice These Principles in all our affairs

All of what we have learned and all that we have said about program and recovery is meaningless if we go out into the world and act like jerks. Living a 12 Step lifestyle means holding oneself to a higher standard, regardless of how others conduct themselves. We don't do this because we're trying to be saints, but because we know leading any kind of lifestyle other than this will put us on the road to relapse.

One of my favorite examples of this was once when I was getting speakers for one of my local meetings. We tried to get people with long-term recovery because it was the meeting that was podcast – and I especially wanted people who "walked the walk." One of my favorite program people is a guy with the kind of recovery I admired. He is a high-powered lawyer, but you'd never know it at meetings. He is very self-effacing, and although he leads a very busy and full life, he still does lots of service in program. When I asked him to speak at my meeting, he said to me, "Sorry John, but your meeting is on Saturday night, and I've made a promise to my wife that Saturday nights are 'our night.'"

To me, this was a perfect example of the second part of the 12th Step. He had made a promise to his wife and that was that. The alternative would be to tell her the meeting took precedence to his commitment to her. So instead of *telling* people how well he worked the Steps, he *showed* people (well me, mainly) that he was working the Steps in all his affairs.

As a child of alcoholics, the worst crime I could commit is to let someone take advantage of me. I went through life so suspicious and untrusting of people. "Fool me once, shame on you" the saying went, and I was going to be sure you wouldn't fool me twice. As a result, I went through life in a defensive crouch. Nevertheless, people *still* did bad things to me from time to time. Living in that defensive way sets up a self-fulfilling prophecy. If you spend your life expecting the worst from people, you will tend to bring that out in them. At the very least, you certainly won't win any congeniality contests.

I don't want to live that way today. Going through life in that defensive crouch – constantly scanning the horizon for possible attacks and slights takes a *lot* of effort. When I drilled down on this behavior in my inventories I realized what was at the bottom of it all – fear. So today, I live a less defensive lifestyle. Does that mean I might get taken advantage of a bit more? Possibly, but that's a price I'm now willing to pay – if it gives me a more serene and happy life.

Living in recovery also means keeping the mirror pointed towards myself. In the past I was quick to see all of your faults and actions, but also quick to justify my own actions. Today, if I have a conflict with someone, I am much quicker to ask myself "okay, what was my part in that?"

The result of all of this improvement is a happier life. Being a happier and more content person, you tend to find people like you more. No longer do I have a lot of the character flaws that used to make me less than desirable to be around. I don't have to be the center of attention anymore and I don't have to correct people when they make misstatements. I can simply be one among many.

Another part of recovery is that I'm *real* today. The person you see is the person I am. The growth is that I am content with who I am – I don't have to play at being someone else for you. Today, I am not afraid of saying I don't agree with you, but I say it in a peaceful and non-confronting way. There isn't a need that I be seen as right and you as wrong, we can just disagree. We may have both found something that works for us but that wouldn't work for the other. In a case like that, we might _both_ be right.

The most important trait I have today that I lacked earlier in my recovery is *compassion*. I have compassion for others, and also for myself. I heard said at a meeting once "Never talk to yourself any worse than you would talk to some child of whom you are fond." Part of my growth is realizing I'm the result of some troubled upbringing and some of the residual "bad learning" may take a lifetime to unlearn.

Once I was able to have compassion for myself, I could have compassion for others. It's easy to have compassion for others when you are simply observing them, or you are interacting with them in a favorable way – but what about the person who is being aggressive towards you? From my dysfunctional family of origin, I was taught that in a confrontation it was important to give as much or more than I got. If you attacked me in any way, I had to make sure you got enough in return to never try that again on me.

Today, if someone is aggressive towards me, I can look at that person with compassion and know that chances are they're hurting inside. As I said earlier, "hurt people hurt people." Also, I know I am a good person, not deserving of any disrespect or derision. I don't have to "buy in" to their assessment of me. If someone starts yelling at you about your ugly green hair, you're not going to get very upset – because you know you don't have green hair. It's the same with having good self-esteem. When a person has that, and feels it at a gut level, others derisions bounces off as if that person *was* telling them they have green hair.

In the end, we're all just little kids running around in adult suits and no one gave us instructions on how to be an adult.

The good news is that there is a manual – or rather a number of manuals. They comprise the literature of the program: the Big Book, the A.A. 12 and 12, and the O.A. 12 and 12. Following the guidelines in these books help me to work at growing up.

Today, I don't need to get in touch with my inner child – I need to get in touch with my inner adult.

Chapter 12 – The Elephant in the Room: Sexuality

Looking back at my thirty-plus years in program, I see that a big topic that "drives" a lot of people's disease – and more importantly why they eventually relapse – is sexuality.

By "sexuality", I mean a great number of constituent parts. While it can be about sex (the physical act), it also encompasses a great many other topics: dating, body image, attractiveness, self-esteem, intimacy (not the sexual type), relationships in general, and of course, love.

These topics each within themselves have multiple levels, just like the food. They are the cause of many relapses and often the core engine of fear that drives some to be chronic relapsers. While part of the chronic slipper wants recovery, another part inside is *terrified of it.* To that side of their brain, recovery might lead to sexuality and intimacy, and that complex component is scary.

The whole "mating dance" involves many facets of all this – topics like rejection, body image, and self-esteem. Body image issues often stem from a childhood where families or other children judged us by our appearance. In school, we had to endure the ordeal of getting chosen for teams (or often *not* getting chosen for teams – or chosen last). This was an essential test of acceptance by others. I remembered that feeling, and some years later when I got to dating age, thought of how it was going to be when I got rejected by someone I liked. Psychic wounds like that often affect our behavior for the rest of our lives – unless we have a program to change it.

In this chapter, I will use the phrase – from time to time – of "the opposite sex" when talking about various topics. Obviously, coming from a heterosexual perspective, it's what I know. Rather than make things grammatically awkward and confusing, I will use this terminology. If you are gay, you might have to make some adjustments in the wording, but it won't be any harder than changing "alcohol" to "food" when dealing with program readings. At the core, there is no difference in the feelings involved, just the gender of the "other" in all of these situations.

Attractiveness

Until I came to program, I had been overweight almost all of my life. When I began recovery and losing weight, I had a huge fantasy built up in my head about what it would be like to be at "goal weight." Just the thought of the phrase "goal weight" came with the singing of a choir of angels in my warped head. Here's what I thought: Once I reached that magic number, I would become self-confident. I would be able to talk suavely to women (probably in a British accent like James Bond), and in fact women would probably be clawing at my ankles when I walked down the street.

The reality of reaching that magic weight was this: I got to goal weight. *Period.* Nothing felt the slightest bit different inside me. I was still terribly shy with women, I didn't like myself any better, and still thought I was ugly and fat. I would focus on the imperfections of my body when looking in the mirror and blow them out of proportion.

As a result of these feelings, I decided that I must not yet be at the correct weight. So I lost some *more* weight. Reaching the new reconfigured goal weight, I saw that I *still* didn't like myself so... I must need to lose a few *more* pounds. For the one and only time in my life, I was going through an anorexic phase. I had people in program coming up to me saying I should *gain* weight. Inside, I took a perverse pleasure in hearing that.

What this taught me – finally – was that all of the things I was hoping would change in me were not really related on a number on a scale. I suppose this is a little like when people say that being rich won't make you happy. The universal response is: "you're probably right, but let me get to be rich first to prove it to myself." I think I *had* to get to goal weight (and then some) to really comprehend that my weight and my self-esteem were not linked.

As a matter of fact, at that point in my life, I was "thin is not well" on the hoof. Yes, thanks to that 26-year old male metabolism I had shed the physical effects of this disease, but was still knee deep in the mental and spiritual morass of the same disease.

It sounds a bit like pandering when I say this at a workshop or retreat, but I truly believe it: "*Women have a harder time with weight loss and sexuality than men do.*" In looking back at my first significant weight loss when I was in my 20s, I don't think I had a clue of my actual attractiveness to women. I had no sisters, was not raised around any women with whom I could talk, so I was naïve to all of the non-verbal communication that goes on between men and women. I understand it a little bit more than when I was younger, but it's still a bit of a baffling road to me – so thank God I'm married and don't even need to think about it as much these days.

Women, on the other hand, are not so lucky. If they reach a normal weight range, they become the unwitting center of attention – wanted and unwanted – almost immediately. They are no longer invisible to men. For some women this attention can be very stressful. The one thing we don't get with attractiveness is the accompanying filter for people we don't want to attract. Wouldn't it be great if you had a filter that made you attractive to *only* the people you wanted to attract? When it comes to the rest, however, *leave me alone.*

Self esteem

The one thing that really attracts people to you is good self-esteem. A person who is comfortable in his/her skin exudes a certain something that people find attractive. I have a friend who I knew from another food program. He was always overweight and had come into that program to drop down from his high of about 500 pounds, which he did. However, I don't think he ever got much below 300. Yet, he was a "chick magnet." He was a comedian and singer, and he was funny, charming and was never without a girlfriend. This drove me crazy because even after years in program (and at a healthy body weight), I remained terribly shy around women. The reason he did so well with the opposite sex, I believe, was that he was raised by parents who never made weight an issue. As a result, he was instilled with a normal self-confidence that I lacked. He was also proof positive to me that weight was only nominally an issue when it came to sexual and romantic relationships.

When I lived in Connecticut, I had a crush on a woman in my home meeting. Everything about her enthralled me. Then she told her story one night, talking in particular how she didn't think she was attractive.

I remember driving home thinking about how we all seem unable to see how others see us. It got me thinking about exactly what it was I found attractive about her. She had a great smile and a great laugh. She was funny, smart, and yes, I thought she was very pretty. Then I thought about what she probably saw when she looked in the mirror in the morning. Almost none of the things I found attractive were things she could easily see in the mirror. She would not stand there and smile, or laugh, or say something witty. It dawned on me that the same was probably true for me. It really hit me that I had to leave that decision (whether or not I was attractive) up to others. It was none of my business.

I remember telling a sponsor I didn't think I was attractive. He asked me, "Are you straight or gay?" When I replied "straight" he said, "So, as a straight man, you have no real idea of what's attractive in men because you're not attracted to men, right?" He was having some fun with me, but I saw his point.

In reality, looks are, of course, totally subjective. I have devised my "98% theory," My "98% theory" says the vast majority of us are in the great 98%. Humanity is divided into three sections: 1% of the people are at the top: absolute gods and goddesses and practically everyone thinks they are good looking. 1% of the people are at the bottom: they are in some way physically deformed. The rest of us fall into the great 98% in the middle – which means some people are going to find us attractive and some people are not.

I can simply look to my own likes and dislikes to see proof of that. There is a certain cover girl model that a large majority of the world thinks is their paradigm of beauty. I don't get it. I don't think she's ugly, but I also don't get any sexual "hit" when I look at her. Conversely, there is a well-known female comic that many people think is not attractive. I am not one of those people. I think she has a great smile, is funny, smart and exudes a "certain something" for me.

The point here is that when I examined my own tastes, I understood that I could only guess at what people found attractive in me. I think at that point I was able to let go of those thoughts and just live life not worrying about my looks and who was or was not attracted to me.

It really does have more to do with what's on the inside than anything else. Having spent the last 15 years in Los Angeles, I found out something about beauty that I used in a script once: *Some of the ugliest women I ever met in L.A. were drop dead gorgeous."*

A lot of people in program are doing what I did at one time: putting their lives on hold until they are "perfect." Of course perfect, like tomorrow, never comes. When I later dug down deeper on that phase of my life, the emotion I found – as is often the case – was fear. If I could convince myself I wasn't perfect and therefore not ready to be putting myself out there, I didn't have to deal with all of the ramifications that come with making that decision to go forth into the dating world. Sometimes I don't want to admit such fears to myself, so it's easier to delude myself with the idea that it's actually a matter of waiting until I'm "perfect," then I'm off the hook on having to take any action.

Before program, when I was approaching a woman I was interested in, it would never have occurred to me that she might be interested in me as well. I was like Oliver Twist walking up with a bowl, asking "please sir, can I have some more?" I felt like a used car salesman that was trying to sell a piece of crap car and was just hoping the person would get it off the lot before it fell apart. After all, once a woman saw the real piece of crap I was (as I saw myself), she wouldn't want to have anything to do with me. That was the depth of my self-loathing – and no amount of weight loss was going to make that go away. That's where the Steps had to come into play.

I had a therapist ask me once: "What do you look for in a woman?" I replied, "Pretty much if she shows *any* interest in me whatsoever." He laughed and told me it was time to start setting the bar a little higher. I had a right to decide what I wanted in a partner too.

One of the reasons I had trouble answering that question about what I looked for in a woman was that there wasn't much *me* in there to begin with. Who was I? Whoever you wanted me to be. You like Chinese Opera? Wow, so do I! You love watching senior golf on television? Me too! I was whatever you wanted me to be. I liked whatever I thought you liked. This was because I was so desperate to be liked and so fearful that any disagreement with you would send you away. I had no intrinsic self-worth. It was sad.

The really embarrassing fact is that the only women I ever approached were ones to whom I wasn't overly attracted. The extra pressure of having to approach a woman who I felt was attractive was too much for me. There's something very sad about that. The reason I was able to get together with one of my girlfriends was that she was the first woman around whom I ever felt reasonably comfortable. She was funny like me and in many ways we were great pals. But I had no ability to approach a really attractive woman.

A few years ago, I became good friends with a woman in L.A. who was very attractive. She had been an NFL cheerleader. She was always complaining about the jerk guys she ended up with. I told her I thought it was because she was gorgeous, and when she dolled herself up even more, she was beyond stunning. I think most guys have some kind of internal scale of who is "attainable" or "unattainable" in the opposite sex. As a result, there were a lot of women "out of my league" and she was one of them. So, in her case, the only guys she ended up with her were egomaniacs that thought they were hot stuff and in turn acted like jerks because they felt they were doing women a favor by dating them.

The other thing about my defenses is that they were highly developed. I was terribly shy, but in a convoluted way. Somehow, I knew that *really* shy people end up having people come up to them at social gatherings in an effort to draw them out. What I would do was to come out to _you_, so that I could set the boundaries. I was a master on so many levels of *seeming* outgoing and gregarious while actually keeping any interaction brief and very shallow. God forbid you – or anyone else – get inside the armor.

I have read for years that women find humor and intelligence one of the most attractive qualities in a man. Well, I have been a professional standup comedian and have a top level IQ – I've even been on Jeopardy! Additionally, I also had (still have, actually) many other qualities that members of the other sex say they want. The one thing I did not have was a good feeling about myself. My self-confidence and self-acceptance levels were just slightly above non-existent.

A number of years into recovery, I still suffered from poor body image and body dysmorphia. I lost the weight on my body *years* before I lost it in my head. I was still a fat guy between the ears. Also, if weight has been an issue your entire life, it's going to have a disproportionate place in your beliefs about your attractiveness. Interestingly, the only person's weight that ever bothered me was my own. Most of the women with whom I have been in relationships have not been happy with their weight. My wife could be 100 pounds overweight (she isn't), but I wouldn't care. When we go out she feels the need to put on makeup. As a guy, I don't understand this exactly, but I have learned that *she* feels better putting on makeup, and since I care how *she* feels, I am in favor of it.

It's still all about how we feel about ourselves – and just putting down the food won't do it. We need to start feeling better about ourselves, and that's where the Steps come in. When you start to feel good about the person you are, you'll immediately become more attractive. Good self-esteem and self-respect comes, as I mentioned earlier, from doing esteemable acts. One of the most important esteemable acts comes from treating yourself well – mainly by staying out of the food and taking care of the only body you'll ever own.

Ironically, the way I got comfortable around women in general was thanks to being in various food programs made up of about 90% women. For shy men, it's a crash course in male/female interaction – and on a much deeper emotional level than the places where single people meet.

Fear of Success – and Attention:

As I said, when it comes to recovery from compulsive overeating, women have it harder than men. Unlike most addictions, _recovery_ from this addiction actually comes with its own set of problems, something not found in most other 12 Step programs.

When I was a young man, my friends and I would see some attractive women as "stuck up." What I came to understand later was these were probably just attractive women who had never figured out how to handle the attention. The result was that they had built a wall of "leave me alone" vibes that made them seem extremely unfriendly. Other pretty girls, on the other hand, had help in learning how to deal with the attention in a more gracious way. This was probably due to having mothers, sisters, or friends that helped them learn how to graciously handle such attention.

Another problem for some people – even me in some cases – was that after a lifetime of being the *rejected* party in dating situations, now I might occasionally have to be the *rejecter*. In my case, sometimes I didn't know how to tell someone they weren't right for me. As a result, I would date that person for way too long when I knew after our first coffee date I wasn't that into them. In the end, I came to understand that if I didn't feel it was right, it was just leading the other person on to not let them know as soon as I realized it wasn't going to work. After all, it would be what I would want for myself if the positions were reversed.

All of this love/hate relationship with attractiveness is, unfortunately, a major cause of recidivism and relapse within food programs. Not only is unwanted attention hard to take, sometimes even *wanted* attention brings with it problems. In the cases of wanted attention, it comes with the added pressure of going on dates, dealing with the possibility of rejection once you really start liking someone, and much more. As a result, often the person who professes to want to be thin and attractive sub-consciously says to themselves "life was a lot easier and simple when I was sitting alone with my goodies watching a movie on a Saturday night."

I saw another cause of relapse a few years back with a woman I sponsored. She had been a "star" in program for a few years, and then lost her abstinence and never regained it for more than a month of two. It wasn't until she told me her story that things became clearer. She was a woman of about 50 who had been heavy her whole adult life. She had constantly tried to diet, but to no avail (the classic pre-program story). Finally, she found program, fell in love with it, and lost all of her weight and kept it off for those years she was abstaining. Then the bottom dropped out of her recovery in an almost inexplicable way. What had happened?

The answer was that reality had begun to creep into her life. Like me, she had all the fantasies of how her life would be when she lost weight. All of her life, that panacea – a fantasy, actually – of how things would be once she lost weight had been in her mind. Now she was at her "goal weight" and had remained there for quite a while. *But she still wasn't getting much attention from men.* Why? Because she lived in L.A. and while she was thin, she was also 50 years old. L.A. is not particularly nice to single 50 year old women. 50 year old men tend to date 40 year old women.

So there she was, as thin as she had ever been in her adult life and her worst nightmare had come true: she was thin and *still* wasn't getting any attention from men. While she could lose the weight, she couldn't lose the years. So not only was she not getting attention from the opposite sex, but she wasn't getting her favorite foods either! As a result, she relapsed. While I tried to work with her, she was never able to string more than a few weeks of recovery together, even as we tried to start working the Steps. She eventually drifted away from the program and I have since lost touch with her.

The point of this last story is that here is yet another reason for either relapse or fear of success. For some, it might be better to not get to goal weight and never have to deal with that scary possibility. Those people may unconsciously choose to live in the "someday" fantasy rather than deal with reality today.

I remember being new to program and also being young and arrogant. I would hear women talk about having trouble dealing with weight loss and being attractive. Many of them talked about the relapses that happened as a result. As a 26-year old man (a boy, in actuality) I would say "These women are never happy! They complain when they're heavy, they complain when they're thin!" Years later, I was married and working on the road as a standup comic. This was one of the times where my food got out of control. It took me a while – and coming off the road – to get my food back in order. It wasn't until later that I realized that I had been dealing with the exact same syndrome those women I had criticized had been dealing with. Being a married man, I wanted to be faithful. On the other hand, being on the road for long periods of time – and also being the center of attention during and after a show – meant that there were opportunities to be unfaithful without very much effort. As a result, subconsciously, I began to eat – partly as a way to make myself less attractive and therefore at less risk of having to deal with "the unfaithfulness question." Be careful what you deride, as I came to learn, because chances are you'll end up having to deal with the same problem some day!

This fear of success begins to melt away when you truly believe in a Higher Power that won't bring you this far only to let you down once success happens. The key is working the program through *all* of the Steps, not just the ones that help you shed the pounds. My sponsee that relapsed, while she had gotten the physical aspect of the disease, had never – in my opinion – expanded her spiritual condition through the Steps. As a result, she had no real support or ability to see a bigger picture – other than her immediate wants and needs. It's quite possible that the man of her dreams was a few weeks away when she threw in the towel. As they say, *"Don't leave before the miracle happens."*

Another problem for some people is the fear around the power of one's sexuality. When those feelings and sexual urges are aroused in us, it sometimes feels like it has a lot of power and might possibly get beyond our ability to control it. It can seem overwhelming. For some, it almost feels like a form of insanity. It is not. Sexuality and arousal is a part of life. In fact, it is part of our biology.

Sexuality

Woody Allen, in a New Yorker article, once asked the question: "Is sex dirty?" The answer, according to Woody was: "only if you're doing it right." This was from the person who made a film called "Everything You Ever Wanted to Know About Sex (But Were Afraid to Ask)." In that film, at one point, the goings-on inside a man's brain are shown during the lead up to sex. It involves a bunch of people – acting as parts of his brain – performing different functions. As the man has performance problems, the reason was found – a minister lurking inside a hidden area of his brain. The point (and joke) here is that when it comes to sex, there is always a certain amount of societal guilt about it.

Whether it was the reluctance of our parents to talk about sex – or even society's taboos about showing anything about overt sexuality – it all leads to the unconscious belief that sex is bad and/or dirty. It might also be one's sexual orientation. For much of history, anything but strict heterosexuality was considered wrong, even sinful. As a result, we get down on ourselves about our God-given sexuality because of inherited hang-ups! The Big Book talks about sex in a much more enlightened way. It speaks of sex being a natural drive and instinct (without it, we – as a species – are not long of this world). Often, as the Big Book also says, we are simply dealing with "instincts gone awry."

For most of us, our first introduction to sex was "sex for one," otherwise known as masturbation. Again, there have been societal and religious restrictions on this. There are also some unfair double standards about this subject between the two sexes.

Masturbation is almost expected from young men, but not for women.

This double standard continues on to the point where people are becoming sexually active. Men who have many sexual partners are mostly not thought of negatively. This view, however, is not often shared when people talk about women. The word "promiscuous" is almost never used in reference to a man. Why? Old beliefs continue to be propagated because of the overall silence – by both sexes – on the topic. There was a time not too long ago that all societies were extremely male dominated. The result of this gender bias probably led to these various double standards – probably conceived by insecure men. This is the 21st century, however, and we are each free to redefine our own standards concerning this subject. The one thing we must not do is anything that will lead us to have to put something on our next 4th Step. When it comes to this subject, listen to that "little voice" inside and remember that we're now trying to lead lives guided by a new way of living.

Then there is the sex act itself. We're not going to get graphic here, but rather let's talk about some of the thorny issues that have to be dealt with when one becomes sexually active. Many of us with current or past weight issues are uncomfortable with our bodies. If we are going to become sexually active, we are going to have to get naked in front of another human being! After all, there is only so much you can do in the dark. There can also be physical scars from our past that we might want to hide. At some point you will need to be able to talk about it with your partner and if things are as they should be, it won't be a problem. We are almost always our own worst critics when it comes to our appearance.

Later, for both sexes, comes the issue of performance – or more often rather performance anxiety. For men, there is the real issue of physical performance. This is one of the few places where men can have a more difficult time than women. Sometimes this lack of physical performance is psychological, other times it's a health problem of a varying degree of seriousness. More often than not, these physiological limitations are simply a matter of blood flow. For those times, however, there are now medications.

Both men and women can have performance anxiety, particularly if one person thinks the other person is more "worldly." Will we measure up to our partner's former lovers? Perhaps we have insecurities about our ability to please the other person. At times we become so involved with making sure the other person is satisfied that sex becomes more of a chore than the pleasurable experience it was meant to be.

There are also legitimate fears involved with sex. For those in the child-bearing years, there is the fear of unwanted pregnancy. In this day and age, there are also the fears of various sexually transmitted diseases. All of these get piled on to whatever previous anxieties might reside in our sub-conscious.

For some people with eating disorders, there are awful specters from the past. They have either been molested or had other unwanted sexual attention foisted on them as children. There is also the case where some women developed earlier than the other girls and had to endure too much sexual attention too soon. This is often the catalyst for many young women gaining weight. The fear of more unwanted sexual attention is too overwhelming for some. Putting on weight can provide "body armor" against the attention – or they can become "invisible" to the opposite sex. There is a school of thought that says that the weight also presents a more formidable presence, which might discourage this unwanted attention. At the other end of the spectrum are anorexic women, who sometimes become thin and "boy like" in another attempt at sexual invisibility.

It's easy to see how stepping into the realm of sexuality can seem like stepping into a minefield. The difference, however, is now we are walking into this arena with our eyes wide open and our heads held high. We are also doing so with some kind of conscious contact with a Higher Power and the belief we can work through all of this. It's also important to remember that we now live in a time where "no means no." You, and only you, get to determine what you will or will not do – and when.

Then there's the matter of sex vs. love. This may come as a shock to you, but men and women are different in how they experience sex. For most women, sex is about intimacy. For men this can also be true, but for some men, sex is often seen simply as a physical act. As I heard one person say, "Sex can often be the *least* intimate part of a relationship." Other men can see it as more intimate, but often not as the special intimacy that many women do. Most guys don't understand why you can't play tennis with a woman one moment, go have sex afterwards, and then go back to playing some more tennis.

For most women, sex is a Rubicon that once crossed, makes the relationship different. While both men and women have the hormone oxytocin, women tend to have more of it. As a result, it works as a "bonding hormone" in women, and it's often released during sex. It explains why women want to spend time together with their partner after the act, while men are either ready to move on – or to sleep. This physical reaction then translates into an emotional one. This is why some men seem astounded when women see a man's infidelity as much more of a betrayal than they do. This is not to say that men don't see infidelity as a betrayal, but their reaction to it is sometimes quite different.

When I completed my sex inventory, one of the things that came up was the times – mostly as a young man in my early 20s – that I hurt someone by quitting on a relationship after a short time – usually after having sex. In looking back on it, part of this was related to my low self-esteem. It never dawned on me that someone could have been hurt when I left. Because I didn't like myself very much, I didn't think my leaving would affect the other person to any extent. Perhaps this is rationalization on my part, I can never be totally sure.

Intimacy and Love

The hardest thing for men to understand is the difference between sexuality and intimacy. Sex can be a block to intimacy. True intimacy means that I have to be willing to be vulnerable and "let someone in." To be naked physically can be hard, but naked emotionally is even harder.

Years ago, I heard a great metaphor for intimacy – the story of the lobster. In nature, the lobster has only one defense against predators – its shell. Yet, once a year it must shed its shell in order *to grow*. Even though the shell is its main defense, it's also an obstacle to growth.

Such is the case with intimacy. We can spend our lives being guarded against being hurt – but to what end? To achieve that, it means never being involved with another person, or going into each relationship in that defensive crouch I mentioned earlier.

Usually that type of attitude makes getting hurt more likely, because who wants to be with a person who is projecting ahead to the end of the relationship?

Another favorite metaphor for allowing oneself to find love, and overcoming the fear of putting oneself out there to the experience, was expressed in a film called "City of Angels." In it an angel, having come to Earth, invites a human to step off a building with him. At first she is dubious (for most people stepping off the top of a building doesn't end well), but then she does it – and is held aloft by the angel. To me, this is the equivalent of falling in love. You have to be willing to deal with the "fear of splat" when "stepping off the building."

Grasping the program and some concept of a Higher Power that is watching over you is the key to finding trust. There's nothing that says working a program will guard you against being hurt. It just assures you that you can get through that hurt and come out the other side – and become a better person for the experience. There is an old program slogan that says "sometimes rejection is God's protection." As with other things in my life, sometimes I am the worst judge of what (or who) is right for me. I have to have the faith that a Higher Power – call it fate if you need to – has my back. The right person for me might then be there for me – mainly because I wasn't involved with the person who rejected me.

I have, at times, called myself "the anti-stalker." I had a highly honed defense mechanism that worked at not only protecting me from hurt by rejection, but protecting me from the possibility of being hurt at all. If I was interested in a woman and asked her out, she might start to say "I can't go out that night, but I'd love to go out some other time." The trouble is by the time she got to the "can't," I was already backtracking saying "that's okay, I just meant for a friend type of date."

Ironically, this type of personality might seem to be the polar opposite of a stalker, but in many ways, those poles curve around and meet. Both my personality – and that of the stalker – cannot bear rejection. The difference was and is how we handle it. The stalker "doesn't take no for an answer," while my personality – also intensely desirous to avoid rejection – denies that I was even really interested. Sometimes I even convinced *myself* of it. As I have said, "the smarter you are, the more convoluted the head games have to get with yourself."

My fear of rejection meant I needed to be 100% sure of _her_ affection before I could even consider having any affection _for_ her. I couldn't even allow myself to feel love and affection until I felt safe.

There's a great scene from Charlie Kaufman's film "_Adaptation_" where one brother makes fun of another for having a crush in high school on a girl named Sarah.

The first brother says: "_I loved Sarah. It was mine – that love. I owned it. Even Sarah didn't have the right to take it away. I can love whoever I want._"

The other brother says: "_But she thought you were pathetic._"

He replies: "_That was her business, not mine. You are what you love, not what loves you. That's what I decided a long time ago._"

That kind of emotional bravery is astounding. To be able to continue to love in the face of rejection is something I know I couldn't do – at least until working the program.

Some people say they want to find someone, but never seem to have the time or ability to put themselves out there. I had a female friend who was always bemoaning her dismal social life, but at the same time she was a workaholic who wouldn't have been able to squeeze in a date if someone asked. At some point, a person has to be willing to make space to have a relationship. One also has to be willing to take a look at oneself and one's lifestyle and ask "is this something another person would really want to be a part of?"

My ex-girlfriend was a therapist. Whenever one of the young female patients complained about not being able to get into a relationship, she had one hard and fast rule – they were _not_ allowed to get any pets. Her main rationale was that it dulls the need to find someone, as we can put our love and affection onto something onto which we project our feelings. We feel that they are reciprocating. I love my dog, but I really get the main thing she sees me as is the provider of food (not that it stops me from fawning over her). Sometimes we find these substitute objects like cats, but that's also a way to feel _just_ good enough to not get over the fear hump and go do something about not being alone. It's like giving up the food/booze – you might need some pain to motivate you into the correct action.

For many years, I had an intense fear of emotional pain. Many years of therapy got me to see this was the result of a messed up childhood. Back then, I experienced considerable emotional pain due to being let down, rejected and hurt by the people that mattered most to me. The hurt was almost unbearable. For many years, I engaged in futile efforts to avoid emotional pain. What I needed to do was to develop a sense of trust in others. If I couldn't trust, how can I be fully invested in a relationship? Having such a damaged trust mechanism would result in me always being on pins and needles waiting for the other shoe to drop and the relationship to end.

A therapist got me to see was that I was still experiencing emotions from the place of that little child. When I was a small child the emotions were huge compared to me, so of course they seemed overwhelming. Now I was an adult, and those emotions were no longer huge – they were normal sized. The feeling that these emotions would overwhelm me to the point of feeling mortal danger was gone. Yes, I might still feel hurt, but it would go away in time. It was all a matter of proportion.

Some people continually make bad choices when it comes to relationships. I have heard women say, "I have a bad people picker." I often suggest to them that perhaps they are thinking of it in the wrong way. Instead of a "bad people picker," maybe they have a broken _filter_. When it comes to a potential mate, who _don't_ they see when they're in a possible meet-up situation? Many people filter out potential partners, often for understandable reasons. We all tend to look past those much younger or older than ourselves. In other cases, the reasons for ignoring possible mates might be more subtle or unconscious. Sometimes people make the snap decision that the person they've just met is boring. Often attraction is based on some allure, which includes a streak of excitement in the other person. Many women profess to liking "bad boys," but then are hurt by them over and over. When women tell me these stories, I remind them that they're called "bad boys" for a reason. Often the kind of "excitement" these women continually look for turns later into a bad relationship. Who needs _that_ kind of excitement?

In the past, my poor body image made it hard for me to accept compliments. When anybody complimented me, I was always quick to add something self-deprecating. What was that about? The root was probably my own self-loathing. I knew the truth about me, I thought. So before you go complimenting me too much, let me disabuse you of the notion that I deserve that compliment. Today, I have learned to smile and simply say "thank you."

Sex in Marriage

I lead a number of retreats each year, and my Saturday night session is usually devoted to sexuality and body image. During these sessions, we send around an "Ask It Basket" so people can anonymously ask questions. One of the subjects that often arises relates to sexuality within a long-term marriage.

In any long-term marriage, no matter how "hot and heavy" the sexual relationship might have been in the beginning, it wanes over time. This has nothing to do with a loss of desirability on the part of anyone, it's just human nature. However, for compulsive overeaters – many of whom dealt with a feeling of not being desirable for a large portion of their life – this can be especially difficult and seen as rejection. The key is to "get out of the rut." As someone who has been in the marriage situation, I know about such things. The rut includes such things as when sex is initiated and what you do when you're involved with it. Sometimes the act itself becomes so rote, that one could choreograph the moves on a sheet of paper in advance. Each person in the relationship needs to get creative about this. If one person or the other in a marriage isn't interested in making this area of life better, the next question is "why not?" This might be fodder for counseling.

It's not always easy to make space for sexual intimacy in a marriage. We lead busy lives, and between work and family, often the only time left is at the end of the day when both partners are exhausted. Like anything else in life, if there is a problem that needs to be fixed, then fixing it must become a priority. All people need to make time for intimacy and sex, and it should be a priority, not an afterthought.

There is also the problem of being unsatisfied with the sex itself. This is often due to one partner or the other not being willing to ask for their needs to be met. The fear that asking might somehow insult the other person is a tough hurdle to pass. In a loving relationship, each partner should be eager to make the other partner happy. Once you've worked the Steps and gotten to the point of realizing you're *worth* speaking up for yourself – in a loving way – you can make inroads into getting what you need.

There is also the program concept of getting out of one's self about these things. Are you feeling not desired in the relationship after a long time together? When was the last time that *you* let your partner know that he or she was desired by you? It's always good to be desired and told so by someone else.

On the other hand, rejection is rejection. When I make advances and my wife says that she is tired and has to get up early, as an adult I can accept this as a viable excuse. However, on some level I still take it a little personally, because basically I'm still just a fat kid inside. As I have learned in program, I let the little kid whine a bit in my head, then I assure him tomorrow is another day and I turn off the light and go to sleep.

I also used to find myself feeling guilty over various sexual thoughts. Having been raised in a slightly repressed home, guilt about sex and sexual thoughts is still something I can grab onto easily. I sometimes have felt guilty about having carnal thoughts about someone other than my wife. I have to remember that those are just _thoughts_. There was a great couple in program that I remember from my days in Connecticut. The wife was a middle aged woman who often made comments about the good looking guys she would see walking by. When I mentioned to her that she was married, she turned to me and said *"Just because you're on a diet doesn't mean you can't look at the menu."* I need to remember that my fantasies are just that – and it is okay, just as long as I don't act on them and give myself something else for my next 4th Step.

There are two other correlations between weight and relationships that I have noticed over the years. One thing is that some people gain weight as a way to test the love of their partner. In many ways it doesn't make sense, but people do it. Working a program and looking at motives in all of one's affairs should bring this out – if the person is aware of it. Sometimes, however, the subconscious rules.

Another thing I see occasionally is people who worked very hard on their abstinence and weight while they were single. Once they have found someone and got married however, they can no longer hold onto their abstinence – or choose not to. The main reason for this has more to do with their *reason* for getting abstinent than the strength of their abstinence. You must work at getting and staying abstinent for *yourself.* That really means delving into the part of the program involved with self-examination rather than solely on the weight. Once you begin to get the benefits of leading an abstinent life, you'll want to do it for its own sake.

Often compulsive overeaters find other eaters as partners, either before or after coming to program. This can become problematic if only one of the two is interested in long term recovery. If suddenly one's binge buddy goes missing, it's easy for the non-recovering person to become resentful. It is also important for the person in recovery to look only at their food and not judge what his or her partner is doing. At the same time, however, there is nothing wrong with letting the partner know (lovingly) that while there won't be any judgment *from* the recovering person, that the same should be true in the other direction.

Sometimes the power of example can help the non-recovering partner find recovery as well. Unfortunately, sometimes it works in reverse, and the person in recovery finds it too hard to be with someone who is still eating. If the abstaining person tends to be co-dependent, it may be hard for him or her to maintain an abstinence knowing the partner is not. Occasionally, due to guilt about their own eating, the non-abstinent partner will, either consciously or sub-consciously, set up situations that can sabotage the recovering partner's abstinence. This is where it becomes vital to develop relationships with people in program that you can talk to when these problems crop up. Sometimes we need to reach out for support when the familial pressure becomes hard to resist. If you find yourself in one of these situations, I would recommend going to as many meetings as possible.

A final word on this subject has to do with program entanglements. As is talked about in the Big Book, it is sometimes the case that *"boy meets girl on A.A. campus"* (or whatever program you're in). While this, in and of itself is not necessarily a bad thing, a rule of thumb is to not be developing romantic relationships with a fellow member with less than a year in program. Allow them the space to work on themselves and their recovery without the extra complexity of a relationship.

Relationships in program are also fraught with possible landmines. First is the aforementioned problem of both people starting the relationship abstinent, then one or the other losing their abstinence. It's important that one's abstinence be strong enough to withstand this development.

Since both people entered the program for other reasons, it's also important that if the relationship does not pan out that both feel free to continue going to meetings and finding recovery. There is nothing worse than an acrimonious program breakup where the people in the relationship have to "divvy up" their meetings like they might do with their joint possessions. Again, the admonition here is: *"tread carefully."*

Relationships

In Al Anon, they have a checklist that points out some problematic relationship situations:
- Do you confuse pity with love, as you did with the problem drinker?
- Do you attract and/or seek people who tend to be compulsive and abusive?
- Do you cling to relationships because you are afraid of being alone?

One of our main problems was mentioned in the A.A. "12 & 12", on page 53 (Step Four):

"The primary fact that we fail to recognize is our total inability to form a true partnership with another human being."

Getting into a relationship means not only sharing your life with someone, but also sharing your character defects. As I often say, my first wife got John 1.0. The next person I was in a long-term relationship with, between my marriages, got John 2.0. Luckily, my wife now has John 3.0 – which is an immensely better version than John 1.0. Thanks to program, the John 4.0 is currently in beta testing.

Here in L.A., an A.A. old-timer and his wife used to run workshops about integrating the program within relationships. In these workshops, they would talk about the idea of utilizing some of the Traditions instead of the Steps. Their primary one was first Tradition: *"Our common welfare comes first."*

This concept meant that the relationship supersedes either person's individual wants or needs. Next, they spoke about how, in any relationship – like in program – there should be no "authority" and reminded us that it resides with our Higher Power, and that we should try to form a consensus about our problems and disputes (the second Tradition). They went on to mention the fourth Tradition – on autonomy – meaning both people should try to keep out of each other's business unless it affected the relationship. Of course, there was the seventh Tradition, in which each person was responsible for their side of the mutual finances (another thorny issue in some relationships).

I feel that couples that make it and are most happy are those that accept each other and don't feel the need try to change their partner. Learning to say "this person has 90% of what I want, I'm happy!" is more of the key to success than "this person has 90% of what I want, and now that I'm in a relationship with them, I can start banging away on the other 10%, to get them exactly the way I want them."

It's like the old joke about the girl who marries the guy, then gets him to change his wardrobe, and then his job, and then how he acts with other people and then she files for divorce. When he asks her why, she says "You're not the person I married!"

Another part of a relationship comes from the program concept of giving acceptance as we would want it given to us. We need to think about our own foibles and quirks, then think of how our partners accept us with them. That's why we need to accept our partners as they are. I heard a story of a 60+ year old man here in L.A. who was asked how he worked his 40 year marriage. He said "I get up every morning, look in the mirror and say to myself, 'You ain't no prize neither!'" Funny, but also true for most of us.

Similar to the concept of "developing and defining a God of our understanding," we should also work on "developing and defining a _relationship_ of our understanding." This means that we need not try to mold ourselves into any of the roles society considers traditional for a relationship. If you want to have the traditional relationship, that's fine, but know that it is not a pre-requisite to having a relationship.

The point is that societal roles are just that – roles defined by someone other than yourself. We can be the men and women God wanted us to be – not what other people want us to be. I work from home, and my wife goes off to work. I joke that I'm the "house husband." It is not really a joke because it's much easier for me – as one who works from home – to do household chores and go shopping during the day. It beats trying to do those things at rush hour in L.A. (actually, *anything* beats doing things at rush hour in L.A.). Who says it shouldn't be that way? Probably a lot of people of my parents' generation would feel that way, but it doesn't matter – the arrangement works for *us*.

The same artificial definitions need not apply to our roles about ourselves either. When I was younger, I tended to get into relationships with women who were not textbook examples of femininity. In looking back at that, I know now that what that was about was that I never felt like a textbook male. I wasn't into football, I like the arts, etc. So if I had a woman that wasn't a textbook female, I didn't have to worry about being the textbook male. This was all borne out of my fear of not "measuring up" to society's pre-conceived notions about masculinity. Again, the program has made me understand – and believe – that I'm exactly the person my Higher Power wants me to be.

Friendship relationships

Finally, in terms of relationships, there are same sex relationships. By "same sex," I'm not talking about gay same-sex relationships, but about men dealing with other men and women dealing with other women in friendship situations.

For a certain number of us, dealing with members of our own sex is sometimes more difficult than dealing with the opposite sex. I often find myself feeling this way. I know a large number of women who prefer hanging out with men – not in a sexual way – than with hanging out with "the girls."

Why? For many of us, as I mentioned previously, it's a matter of not feeling like we "fit in" with societal norms for what "girls" (women) and "boys" (men) are supposed to be like, enjoy talking about, etc. In looking at this, I feel a lot of this came from an earlier, formative time – such as high school. Adolescents are all feeling their way into adulthood and often the insecurities about themselves cause them to turn outward and become critical of other people. This is especially true of those whose manner makes them stand out as "different." I know that I fell into that category while growing up. Some of those taunts, I believe, were what led me to feel "less than" – especially in my role as a man – for many years. I have been told that this same taunting was true for girls of that age. If some of your main formative experiences about yourself were negative ones inflicted by members of your own sex, why *would* you want to have much to do with them, especially in a group setting?

In some gatherings that are either all men or all women, there is a decent amount of comparison and subtle competition that goes on right under the surface. We do it concerning others, but mainly about ourselves and how we compare to others. In the past, I often compared myself unfavorably to my fellow males. In many such situations, I might compare favorably with 9 out of 10 of my fellow men. Will I see that fact easily? No. I will invariably end up comparing myself to the 1 out of 10 against whom I fall short. Why? To fulfill that negative script that has been embedded in my head since childhood. The reality is that we all compare favorably to people in some areas, and unfavorably in other areas. Almost none of us compare unfavorably to anybody in all areas of our lives.

As one of my favorite program speakers says, *"the shortest route to insanity travels through comparison."*

The important thing still comes back to my favorite quote from the A.A. Big Book: *"When I criticize you or me, I'm criticizing God's handiwork. I'm saying I know better than God."* Just like the program teaches me to accept life on life's terms, I need to accept *myself* on God's terms. I have learned to take the foot off the back of my own neck and accept that I am a human being. In other words, I learned to stifle the mental chatter about myself and got on with living my life for myself, not others.

Chapter 13 – Stopping your next Slip, or are you already in it?

Compulsive eating is cunning, baffling, and powerful because it uses self-deception, self-delusion, justification and rationalization to attack us. Part of the problem of trying to get better in recovery is that the majority of the character defects that we have need to lose or reprogram won't happen until the food is put down and we've started working the Steps. Meanwhile, some of those self-same defects are screaming at us to _not_ put down the food. Sometimes the disease, through these defects, tells us that no matter what the program tells us, there _is_ an easier, softer way out there – we just haven't found it. Other times it convinces us that we do have control and we will exercise that control over the food – tomorrow. Of course, this is the disease's main job – to get us to not put down the food – for at least one more day. These are also some of the same thoughts our disease puts in our heads to get us to give up our abstinence and relapse. If you are new to program, these thoughts might very well be the case on a daily basis.

Every addict is susceptible to relapse, if the circumstances are right. The more overall recovery, the more "insurance" you have against a relapse, but there's still no guarantee it cannot happen. Any addict, put under enough pressure, can – and will – revert to type. I've heard it said that for every year of recovery, you get one _second_ to reconsider picking up that first bite. I'm not sure that's the correct ratio, but I agree with the intent – and that more time in program allows you to better see your options.

If you're already in a 12 Step program for food and are in the middle of a slip, I can relate. I was there too. When I look back on it though, I now tend to call it a relapse rather than a slip. There's something remarkably passive about the word "slip." It tends to infer that there was nothing leading up to it and – whoops – there was cake in my mouth! This was hardly the case, and there were certainly warning signs leading up to my relapse.

If you are in a 12 Step program and are starting to feel like your food is getting out of control – surprise, you are probably already in what might be considered a "slip." If you have a flexible food plan, it's very easy for the weight to start creeping back on while you continue to tell yourself that you're abstinent and working a good program. Of course, the truth is that *you* are not telling yourself this, *your disease* is – as it often does – to reassure you that you don't have a problem.

The sad fact is that we all want to think we're the smartest we've ever been at this exact moment, but the reality is that sometimes we go backwards – without realizing it. This disease is insidious and can wheedle its way back into our lives in the most camouflaged of ways. The longer we are in program, the more camouflaged the slide has to be so that we don't recognize that it's happening.

Chronic slippers are common in the various food programs. They come into program, have some initial success and then lose their abstinence. They then spend years trying to get their abstinence back, but to no avail. This is what happened to me early in my recovery.

As I mentioned in my story, when I first came into program, I was "struck abstinent." I was on a pink cloud and losing all my weight – at age 26 – could not have been easier. Then I lost my abstinence – and spent a few years slipping and sliding before I got back on track.

This is a classic program tale. Like all of the diets that worked once for me (then stopped working) before program, the same thing happened *within* program. This was because I had treated the program like just another diet, and while it worked for a while – like all of my other diets – it was doomed to eventual failure. All I had done was the diet, and without doing all of the work in program, there was no hope of any long term recovery.

To those who are in that constant slipping cycle, getting and staying abstinent seems like an insurmountable task. Perhaps it seems so hard because of the way recovery is being approached. One of the things we have to admit is that no matter how long we have been doing it, we are not doing it right – at least not at current time. It is also possible that we have *never* done it right and have just been lucky up until the relapse commenced. Sometimes we have to "tear down the building" and start all over again.

Getting abstinent is often very hard – especially after a prolonged relapse. Abstinence does get easier, if you stick with it. The process is not unlike pushing a stopped car. If you've ever had to push a stopped car, it takes a lot of effort to get it moving initially. After that, it takes a lot less effort to _keep_ it moving. The trouble with constant slipping is that it is like working really hard to get the car moving – only to let it then roll to a stop again just when less effort was right around the next corner. When you are constantly doing the hardest part of abstinence over and over, it's easy to get discouraged!

The other problem with constant slipping is that it never lets you get to the point where you can begin to change the things that are leading to your next slip. If your entire recovery life is spent on just staying abstinent – and not getting to work on the underlying root causes – it's only a matter of time before you're out eating again.

It's hard to see those secondary characteristics driving the "relapse engine." If all you've done is put the food down, it's like taking a car whose throttle is stuck and racing like crazy and throwing the car into neutral. You now have a car that is less dangerous – for the moment. A car with a racing engine, however, is only a slight nudge of the transmission away from being a dangerous flying object. The _other things_ (besides putting down the food) are the key to turning that racing engine off – and working toward dismantling that engine as much as possible. That's where the Steps come in.

A chronic slipper that is currently abstinent has to ask him or herself a very important question: _how is this time in program going to be different?_ Is it really different from the numerous times they have been abstinent in the past, or are they just on another "in" phase? As I heard someone say once about a chronic slipper, "He goes out a lot because he comes back so well."

If you are a chronic slipper, or are currently in relapse, and have looked at the table of contents and jumped to this chapter, I understand why. This kind of behavior is exactly part of the problem. It's about looking for the shortcut to getting abstinent. I'm sorry to say, there is no short cut. I have written extensively in this book the exact details about how to go about getting out of a relapse – and staying abstinent permanently – but it involves starting this book from the beginning. As I said once to a chronically slipping sponsee, "You don't want to _get_ abstinent, you want to _be_ abstinent – but without having to do what all the other people have to do to get abstinent." I understand, because that's also part of the disease – _it's what the disease is telling us to do._ The disease is screaming to you that there's an easier, softer way than the path of true recovery – or at the very least a shortcut. However, the truth is that the disease is telling the person in relapse this not because there really is an easier, softer way. The disease really doesn't want the food addict to get better and knows that shortcuts are the longest way to the goal.

The Rubber hits the Road: What to do when the urge to eat hits

I heard someone say at a meeting once: "at the point when I relapsed, my abstinence had deteriorated to a "white knuckle" abstinence, so it was easier to just go eat." I remember thinking that while a "white knuckle" abstinence is clearly not the optimum existence, it still beats getting back into the food. The reality is that if one gets back into compulsive eating, eventually that person will want to get abstinent again, and at some point in those future early days, he or she will _still_ have to deal with a "white knuckle" abstinence _again_ for a period of time.

For all of our intellect and program talk, I find it amazing sometimes that people don't understand something I heard early on in program: *"We don't eat no matter what."* I remember another, more jaded phrase: "We don't eat even if our ass falls off." I'm not exactly sure how that latter one works, but I get the intent.

The problem I had when I was dealing with slipping after my first "pink cloud" abstinence was that I had no idea how to handle that overwhelming urge to eat. The first abstinence had been such an effortless "grace" abstinence, it never dawned on me that there might be times when I would have to deal with the disease *screaming* in my ear. As a result, I ate almost every time that obsession hit. It brought up the question: how truthful was I being when I said I was *willing to go to any lengths* when it came to my disease?

What I had come to feel – mostly from the experience of always relenting to my disease's ceaseless urging to eat was – that even though I might hold out for a while – once that obsession started, it was only a matter of time before I picked up. It was, after all, the only way to make that urge go away. This conclusion was based on one-sided data, since my experience had only been one of giving in to the disease. I had never explored any alternatives, mostly because my disease had convinced me to not even try.

What I learned later was that there were other, healthy ways to make that urge abate. It involved, however, my being willing to have an emergency plan ahead of time. I spoke about this in depth in the section on the "Action Plan" section of the Tools.

I needed that list of phone numbers I could call at any time of the day or night (some people available late, others available early). More importantly, however, was the *willingness* to call those people when my disease was imploring me to not call. The disease would use the excuse that I would be bothering the people, when the truth was that this was the only way to convince me to go eat. Besides, if I got someone on the phone, they might actually talk me down and I might not eat – which was the last thing my disease wanted me to do.

The commitment to *going to any lengths* to not pick up that first bite is crucial. If you can believe it to the core of your soul, it will go a long way to making the urge not come up at all, or be significantly weakened. If I've truly made the commitment, some of the force behind that overwhelming urge will often dissipate with the disease's thought process being "why bother... he/she will only start calling people and make the urge go away."

As I said earlier, I believe abstinence is a gift from my Higher Power, but we – as compulsive eaters – choose to give it away. Once given away, we can never be sure that we will *ever* get it back again. Such is the true nature of powerlessness. That reality of powerlessness, however, is the last thing our disease wants us to think about when it's doing a full court press to get us to compulsively eat again. It wants us to believe that "I'll start again tomorrow" lie.

To those who are still on the agnostic side of the belief spectrum, I would offer this advice if the overwhelming urge to eat hits. *Pray.* This need not be a formal prayer like you might have learned as a child – or one about which you have read. It can simply be something like *"I really want to eat right now, and I need some help against this unrelenting disease."* Even if you think it is total bunk, what do you have to lose? Perhaps the act of asking is the way of fighting the disease. And if it does work – as I think it will if you ask sincerely – it might give you that little mustard seed of faith that could lead to a belief in a Higher Power that is there to help you conquer this disease – a day at a time.

Dealing with Relapse – the 12th Step Within

Within O.A. and other food programs, there is the concept of "the 12th Step Within." This means reaching out to people who are in relapse within program and being willing to offer them help. During my bad slip, when I was gaining weight like crazy in front of my fellow program members, not one person came up to ask me about it. As a hardcore member in L.A. says, "sometimes we hug each other to death."

For all of us, weight and/or weight gain was a source of shame in our lives. For this reason, few program members are willing to go up to a fellow member and say "Hey... I see you've gained some weight, is everything okay?" _Let me explain why we should._

In food programs, it's not about the weight like in A.A. it's not about your breath. What I mean by that cryptic phrase is that if someone in A.A. came into their home meeting with booze on his breath, it would become about his breath. Weight is the "booze on our breath" in food programs. The fact is that back in that A.A. situation, nobody would wag a finger at the person, or shame him, but rather would say something like, "*I can't help but smell booze on your breath. Is there anything I can do to help you?*"

Yet, within the compulsive eating community, confronting a member about their weight gain is an almost unheard of behavior. I think this is because many of us *say* compulsive eating is a disease, but instead – at some level – see it as a moral failing. If we truly saw it as a disease, we'd be more than willing to approach that person to offer help.

If I was talking to a friend, and as he turned to walk away, I noticed a nasty black mole on the back of his neck – in a place he couldn't see it – wouldn't I say something to him about it? In program, we will watch people gain 40-50 pounds in front of our eyes and not say a thing! In a way, we are colluding with their disease's denial mechanism. I say this as someone who has been just as guilty of this action as others. The concept of the "12th Step

Within" is being willing to reach out to those in relapse and offer help.

To this end, many Intergroups have now set up "12th Step Within" committees that offer workshops and offer help to those struggling in the program. A few years ago, the biggest 12 Step food program, O.A., changed its definition of abstinence in an effort to get people thinking about their own behavior in program. O.A.'s definition of abstinence now says: *"Abstinence in Overeaters Anonymous is the action of refraining from compulsive eating and compulsive food behaviors <u>while working towards or maintaining a healthy body weight</u>. Spiritual, emotional and physical recovery is the result of living the Overeaters Anonymous Twelve-Step program."*

The main reason for this change, I believe, was to dissuade those gaining large amounts of weight from considering themselves abstinent. While recovery is not just about losing weight and maintaining weight loss, neither is it realistic to deny this aspect of recovery. A 12 Step program's continued existence relies on attracting new members who see recovery in action. If those new people see a room full of significantly overweight people who are not losing any weight, it will be hard to convince them that true recovery can be found in that program. As I said in the chapter on the 12th Step, one of the main ways we can be "carrying the message of recovery to those who still suffer" is to be powers of example ourselves – and this means being at, or moving toward, that healthy body weight.

The most important thing about dealing with relapse within program is our ability to *tease the disease away from the person.* Just like religions say "hate the sin, but love the sinner," so should we be willing to fight the disease, but not the person suffering from that disease. To this end, we shouldn't be prevented from helping a fellow compulsive eater out of fear of being in an uncomfortable situation. While it might be uncomfortable in the moment, it might just possibly save their life.

Chapter 14 – Two Last Important Topics

Getting Outside Help

For many of us, getting outside help from the mental health professions is a perfect adjunct to our program of recovery. In many places in A.A. literature, the newcomer is constantly reminded that *"we are not professionals."* Nor should we be expected to act as professionals. We're just here to share our experience, strength, and hope.

A lot of the emphasis heard in the rooms of the program is on the physical and spiritual aspects of the program, and often the emotional (or mental) component gets left by the wayside. This aspect is particularly important to address as many of us began our compulsive eating behavior to avoid emotions that felt too overwhelming. It's important to realize that the laws of psychology don't stop when we walk through the doors of a 12 Step program. As a result, some of us need help that program, the 12 Steps, and a sponsor alone cannot provide.

Bill Wilson, founder of A.A., suffered from depression his entire life. He sought outside help and recommended it heartily to others in A.A. He even corresponded with famed psychiatrist Carl Jung. I can tell you from personal experience that therapists have helped me immensely – once I stopped drinking and using food to medicate myself. As much as sponsors can help in many day-to-day problems, a trained professional can usually see things a few layers down that a lay person cannot.

The key, of course, is to not be currently active in the addiction. I have a good friend that is a "circuit speaker" in A.A. who constantly derides therapy. He says, "I spent thousands of dollars on therapists and none of them got me sober." I always reply, "Of course! You were actively drinking and chances are you were either in those sessions with diminished capacity or lying about the extent of your drinking." That's what we addicts do, after all.

Those that believe that the Big Book and the 12 Steps are the alpha and omega of existence are very short sighted. There are numerous hardcore 12 Step groups in various programs that tend to deride both therapy and medicines that help those with mental problems. While I don't disagree with the general ideas of what they say, to them there is nothing the Big Book cannot cure. I have joked that a person could walk into one of their meetings with a compound fracture of the leg – the bone sticking out of it – and someone would say to them "read page 66 in the Big Book." No!!! Get to an Emergency Room!

I have heard numerous stories of fundamentalist 12 Steppers telling their sponsees to stop taking their bipolar drugs only to have that person commit suicide. In terms of drugs dealing with the physiological aspects of behavioral problems such as depression, all science is trying to do is get the patient to the same baseline everyone else has. It's hard enough to deal with addiction without having to start from below ground.

What I learned in therapy was that while I was gifted with a great brain that can think its way out of a number of complex problems, some areas were outside the realm of logical thought. I overused my intellectual capacity when I couldn't handle my feelings. Getting in touch with my feelings was something that was not taught to me by my family of origin – in fact feelings were actively shunned.

When, as a kid I would have feelings that were not always logical, I would be told: "It's stupid to feel that way." When I left home, I took that "mind over feelings" mentality out into the world. As a result, I didn't have a good understanding or connection with my feelings. Often, I would only become aware that I was upset when I noticed I was acting strangely. What I understand today is that my feelings are my feelings, and they are often divorced from logic. Sometimes my feelings come from that 5 year old child inside me. I can look at those feelings as an adult and want to dismiss them, but they are still valid. If I don't learn to acknowledge them instead of glossing over them with intellect, I am missing something. It's like sewing up a wound without cleaning it out first. It might look better in the beginning, but somewhere down the line it's going to be a lot worse.

This is especially true when something emotionally jarring happens. I need to be able to stop and instead of analyzing it with *thinking*, ask myself "How am I *feeling*?" That's where a therapist has been of the most help to me – to help this child of repressed parents learn how to do as an adult what children of well-adjusted parents learn at a young age.

Often incidents that happen in the present are tied back through the fabric of time to some past event. This connection heightens the feelings and often our reaction to the incident is out of proportion to the incident itself. As the program phrase goes, "If it's hysterical, it's historical." This is another area where a trained, objective professional can be of immense help in putting these events in perspective and historical context.

All of us have "hot buttons," things that really bother us more than they bother others. For me, it's being dismissed. If I get a chance to express my thoughts and you totally disagree with them and overrule me, I'm fine with it – as long as I got to have my say. If you won't let me have my say and dismiss me and my opinions as irrelevant, my blood starts to boil. In looking closely at this with a therapist, I was helped to see that this overreaction to a common occurrence that happens to people all the time goes back to my childhood as the child of alcoholics. Having parents that were totally self-involved and who cared little for my needs and/or opinions on major life decisions makes today's dismissals bring up the feelings of yesterday's frustrations.

Have you ever had an immediate like or dislike of someone? If so, there's a good chance that they probably remind you of someone from your past. I experienced this first-hand once, when I was introduced to someone in program and had an immediate, visceral dislike of him. After I walked away, thanks to program I tried to examine _my_ part in the situation. As far as I could see, there was no logical reason for the dislike. Thanks to a therapist, I was able to see that while this person didn't _look_ like my father, he had a lot of the same mannerisms as my father, and thus reminded me of him – hence my reaction. I had to smile once I realized this, and my program compadre and I have since become good friends. This was another example of things that, with all my program and intelligence, I couldn't see and where outside help was of immense benefit.

Switching addictions

One of the things I have seen a lot of in 12 Step programs are people who put down one substance only to pick up another substance or addictive behavior. Food is often the second addiction for people who are giving up drinking or drugs. For those of us for whom food was the main addiction, a secondary addiction might be spending, or sex, or any one of numerous substance or process addictions.

These various addictions are all just roots of the same tree – a soul sickness that can only be cured with the application of the 12 Steps of recovery. If you decide to simply treat the symptom and not the underlying causes of your addiction, you're setting up either an inevitable relapse or a turn to another addiction. If you cut back on the branches of a tree, it immediately begins to grow new ones, as it needs to "feed" itself. The same is true with addictions. If the Step work doesn't get done, the addiction will find other ways to "feed itself." If the pressure builds up enough in an addict, the disease will find another way to dissipate it – _unless_ you do the inner work.

At the bottom of addictions in many of us is what I call "fear of dead air." In the radio business, "dead air" means silence – especially prolonged silence. For many of us who have been holding onto various "demons," the last thing we want is to be alone with our thoughts. Often, this leads to the urge to turn to anything that fills that void. This can be another substance or different addictive activity, or even just an unrelenting urge to constantly be active and never slow down.

If you are already involved in a second addiction, you need to get help for it immediately, or all of the work done in the first program is in peril. I remember hearing a particularly uncensored old-timer telling a group of O.A. people – many of whom were long-time members of A.A. – an uncomfortable fact: "If you are a compulsive eater and an alcoholic," he said. "And you've given up drinking but not compulsive eating you're not sober – just dry. Sobriety isn't a matter of how much alcohol is in your bloodstream. Read what it says in the Big Book. The Big Book says sobriety is '_soundness of mind_.' How can you have soundness of mind if you're acting out – and self-medicating with another substance?"

I love the phrase "self-medicating," as it perfectly describes the relationship most compulsive eaters have with food. Normal eaters, even ones that like food a little too much, eat for the taste and the desire to stop hunger. Compulsive eaters, however, use food in a pharmaceutical way, to alleviate uncomfortable feelings.

One of the hardest questions we have to ask ourselves is, "Have I switched addictions?" At first, the answer might seem to be "no," but it might be worth your while to ask yourself a question: "Is there anything I'm doing in my life that is not in moderation?" For some it might be shopping, for others sex, gambling, or (for those previous non-drinkers) drinking. I have a friend who was not part of a 12 Step program, but was a compulsive eater that got one of the many forms of stomach surgery. In my mind, that simply treats the symptom, which often morphs into another symptom. In her case, within a few months of the surgery – at 50 years of age – she went from being a moderate drinker to a full-blown alcoholic.

Again, your answer to the above paragraph might be "nope, not me!" Let's move to some more benign behaviors not often associated with addiction, but which are – more and more – being identified as examples of "addictive behavior." Some of us throw ourselves headlong into work, keeping late hours, and not living a full life. Again, as is said in various pieces of program literature "we don't live to recover, we recover to live."

Do you surf the 'net for hours on end? How about watching TV for most of your waking hours? After my father quit drinking (not because he wanted to, but due to a mild stroke), his life became totally about smoking and reading fiction books. I even know someone who began chewing so much gum that she got herself sick.

If any of these behaviors describe a part of your life, you might want to consider that you are still not going through life truly clean and sober. While this book is dedicated to working on compulsive eating, there is also an assumption that all other addictive behaviors have been addressed as well. Without living life free of all substances and addictive behaviors, we will never get the full effect of working the Steps. It might very well eventually lead to relapse.

The reality is that for some of us, life is hard to do without something to protect us. Having no more substance or behavior to act out with means we need to deal with life on life's terms. This gets easier with more recovery, but in the beginning it may be hard – and the temptation to find another way to "bleed off some pressure" will be great. It's important to remember that some emotional discomfort is the price we will have to pay for the recovery. Besides, it isn't avoiding that pain, just delaying it. In many ways, continuing to act out is only adding to the existing pain by adding more things to feel bad about. An old timer says "Fight for your right to be uncomfortable."

If you continue, the hard work pays off.

Chapter 15 – The Final Gift (What's in it for me?)

The main reason most people come into a 12 Step program for food is to lose weight. More than just losing the weight you had on your body at that moment, you also wanted to stop both the up and down cycles, and also to be rid of the constant obsession with food.

Even in my twenties, I was tired of that life-long struggle with my weight and my relationship with a substance most people don't give a thought to once they push away from the dinner table. Today I have a relationship with food that is *close* to that of "normies." I would like to say that food thoughts never enter my head, but that would be a lie. Thanks to working the program, I have been able to make the food "right sized" in my life and it takes up a whole lot less of my brain space than it used to.

The side effect of the lifting of the food obsession was a lower, dare I say "normal" healthy weight. I walk down the street now without people looking at me as if I were a freak. I have relationships now with people, not just one with the TV and the refrigerator. I am married. I am happy, and I lead a relatively contented life. While I will occasionally get annoyed at everyday things, they don't stay with me for weeks on end like they used to. In general, "The Promises" have come true for me.

I think all of this was a gift from my Higher Power, but I also believe it was my duty to meet him (her? it?) halfway. I needed to be willing to go to any lengths, not only to not eat, but to then do the other things I was told I needed to do to recover. This means that sometimes it is tough. In the beginning, just not eating at night was tough. Later on, continuing with the Steps, especially the 4th and 9th Step, was tough. Now I can see that it was all worth it. I am a better person today. I do not spend my days in that prison of self I lived in constantly, and that is wholly due to the program, the Steps, and the Big Book of Alcoholics Anonymous.

It's important to realize that getting out of ourselves and being more concerned with the welfare of others than ourselves is not necessarily inbred in human beings. We are the descendants of those who, in the past, did a better job of looking out for themselves than the other guy did. It's possible that some of us can trace our blood lines back to some caveman who shoved his buddy down so the saber toothed tiger would eat the buddy instead of him. Self-preservation is the main way our species has continued to thrive. Now the 12 Steps are telling us to forget all that for the sake of our serenity. Meanwhile, the rest of the world doesn't have to play by those same rules. So, in a way, we're holding ourselves to a higher standard. We must remember that we do this to be relieved of our disease's symptoms – a day at a time.

Let me talk about the removal of the obsession with myself.

I always thought I was special, that I somehow was entitled to things over and above everyone else. I felt entitled as a way to make up for how I felt shortchanged in my life. There used to be a TV commercial in which a guy was driving all alone on a highway. Above him, the lit sign said "Bob's Road." That was what I expected out of life. I wanted traffic out of my way and every light to be green. One of the things that made a light bulb go off on this subject was reading an Al Anon pamphlet called "A Checklist to our Emotional Maturity." In it was this line: *some adjustment for the convenience of others is necessary.* What a concept – but one I now understand. As a result, I am now more philosophical when the light turns red and other people get to go instead of myself. Ironically, it was *always* the case that I had to sit at those red lights, only now I am accepting it. The result is a much more serene life.

Another problem with being in the whirlpool of self is that you take everything personally. If someone cuts me off on the road, he was doing it to me personally. No he wasn't – he was just oblivious. As I said before, *"Never attribute to maliciousness that which is more likely attributed to cluelessness."* Translation: sometimes people are dumb and inconsiderate, but it's not about you – it's about them. It's only your problem if you don't realize that.

Continued recovery and working the Steps has multiple rewards. It helps in so many more areas of your life than you had ever expected when you walked through the doors the first time. When I was new to my first program, I read something called "The 20 Questions" in the Connecticut state meeting directory. It asked questions to determine whether you had a problem with drinking. Most of them were fairly obvious, like "Has alcohol ever caused you problems in your life?" One caught my attention more than the others. It said "Do you start projects that you never finish?" This one intrigued me enough to go ask my sponsor what this had to do with alcoholism. He said "We addicts are immature people, and want immediate gratification. When we can't get it, we quit. The trouble is that many of the things in life worth doing do take time and effort and we can't easily endure that time frame."

That one hit me like a ton of bricks.

It was true what they told me, "If you work these Steps, they'll help you in many more areas you had never thought of." I *wish* I had worked more on the Steps earlier in my life. Yes, I had stayed sober, but I was my own worst enemy in many areas of my life for many years into that sobriety. My character defects – things that had been survival techniques in an earlier time – worked against me and kept me back in so many ways. In confrontations in my earlier careers, I had to win each argument – even when letting the other person win would have furthered my cause much more effectively.

When I find myself in a disagreement or confrontation now, I have compassion for another. I can more easily see their side of the argument, even when I think they're wrong. When someone acts angrily toward me, I can realize they're upset and I care about that. As a result, I don't have to zing back and escalate the situation.

The words of that old timer when I was first sober constantly come back to me: *"If you are right, you have no need to be angry; if you are wrong, you have no right to be angry."*

There are many things that can and will affect my serenity. It's my job to be aware when this is happening and to remember the way program teaches me to deal with them. It is often not easy to remember this in the moment, but there is definitely truth in the truism: "*You* don't make me angry – *I* make me angry." It's ironic that I came into this program to lose weight – and I did. But the most important weight I lost was atop my shoulders.

Another part of growth in working the Steps comes in the concept of "moderation in all things." I used to say "anything worth doing is worth overdoing." It's a funny line, but today I realize it came from a life of dysfunction. Moderation in all things is today the ideal towards which I strive.

It's great to be in program and do service, for example, but it's not good to have 16 sponsees. Our lives should be about living. Meetings are for becoming better people out in the world. The goal should not be about only going to meetings. If you can't figure out how to do this, talk to your sponsor about it.

Today I understand that everyone has a Higher Power and it's not my job to take up the slack for *their* Higher Power with my will and control issues. I have a full time job taking care of me. When I have finally gotten my life perfect, then I can start working on your life.

Self-acceptance is another important thing I have gained over the years. I'm a human being and all of my study of the Steps and the Big Book has only reinforced that fact. I needed to learn compassion for myself because I'm a work in progress. I am the product of a childhood nobody should have to have lived. The compassion for myself now comes with an eye towards that frightened little kid that lived a long time ago. He has grown up physically, but in many ways he has a long way to go before his emotional age catches up with his physical age. An interesting thing happened once I learned to do that: becoming less judgmental about me meant I could become less judgmental about you. Again – the path to more serenity.

For many years, I was terrified of losing my uniqueness. I felt I was a rebel and that there was a large mass of humanity that was sheep-like and uniform and I wanted no part of it. Today, I see that was a distorted perception. Perhaps to my view humanity seemed uniform, but it was not. We are all unique and I finally see that. I needed at one time to squash my feelings of inadequacy with a belief that I was the one making myself different from society as a whole. In doing that, I didn't have to look at how I compared with others – because somewhere inside, I knew the awful truth that I was "less than" and defective in so many ways. Today, I realize that I am one among many – and that's just fine for me.

I will reiterate something I said earlier in this book: all of this work, the 12 Steps, the Big Book, the meetings, the program – when boiled down to its simplest form is found in the Serenity Prayer: *"God, grant me the Serenity to accept the things I cannot change, courage to change the things I can, and the wisdom to know the difference."*

I also remember those words of my old sponsor who taught me "... *everything from the skin outward are things you cannot change. Everything from the skin inward are things you can change."* I owe him a debt of gratitude for making that difference so easy to understand.

This book has been about integrating the ideals of the Steps and the Big Book into our lives. *Ideals* is the key word. We must stop beating ourselves up for not meeting program concepts that are ideals. Instead we try to learn from our experiences when we fall short of those ideals and continue to strive to get closer to meeting them.

My recovery has given me a greater ability to be in touch with my feelings. For many of us – especially those of us with high intelligence – we relied on our intelligence at the expense of our emotions and feelings. It seems to me from my observations that this is especially true for men. I read an excellent book about men and emotions entitled: "*I Don't Want to Talk About It,*" a perfect title for the subject. For many of us men, we are taught not to cry, not to show emotion, not to feel. This is denying human psychology and is doomed to failure. Luckily, recovery in a 12 Step program guides me away from such flawed thinking.

Working a 12 Step program doesn't promise a perfect life without troubles and pain. What it does guarantee is that you will survive, even thrive afterwards and possibly see later in retrospect that what happens can be beneficial to you in the long run. As it says in "The Promises": *"We will intuitively know how to handle things that used to baffle us."* We will learn to fight our tendency to want to retreat when things get scary, but trust in a Higher Power instead. The result is we will get *through* things instead of trying to avoid them. Getting through problems is often a way of figuring out how to not go through them again.

When I was new to my first program, everything in my life was wrapped up in drama. I felt like I was in a small life raft being bounced around in an ocean storm. It was all I could do to hang on and not let the problems overwhelm me. When I looked over at the old-timers in program, I saw people going through things way worse than anything facing me. They were going through those problems with grace. I wanted what they had. To me, instead of being bobbing life rafts, they were like ocean liners cutting effortlessly through the waves.

Having reached the point where I've become an old-timer, I've made an outstanding discovery. There's nothing that's going to come down the pike that is going to destroy me. It might annoy me, it might require more effort than I want to go through, but it will not be insurmountable. As a result, I almost never reach the levels of desperation and anxiety that used to plague me in my early recovery. I have come to realize that I've become one of those ocean liners. Now that I've gotten there and see it from the direction of looking outward from it not inward toward it, I realize something else: the reason I'm a steady ocean liner is that I'm an ocean liner *made of mesh*. As result, while it seemed like the old-timers were plowing through the waves, the opposite was actually true: the reason the sailing was so smooth is that *the waves are going through us.*

A few years back, I heard a speaker say something that has helped me greatly ever since. She said *"If you have a problem that can be solved by writing a check, you don't have a problem."* I realize that the key thing here is having the money to cover the check, but then I have to ask the question: "How much is my serenity worth?" Nobody likes to spend extra money, but if it means I stop devoting extra time and effort – both physically and emotionally – to the problem at hand, isn't it worth it?

"We have ceased fighting anything and anyone."

This is the main gift of the program – serenity and happiness. It took me years of looking backward to know that serenity and happiness was what I was trying to achieve with food, alcohol, and any other mind-altering substances I could get my hands on.

That main gift of serenity, coupled with not having to haul around an extra 100 pounds every day, keeps me coming back. I also realize that at my age, I've used up all of my "get out of hell free" cards. There's nothing less healthy physically than continuing to keep going up and down in weight. More importantly for me is remembering that awful feeling I had when I was acting out with the food, but knowing at the same time that there was a better way. I could not have felt worse about myself than I did at that time. I knew the food had taken over and was calling the shots in my life, and I hated it.

It's important for me to remember the bad times with the food, because when my disease comes a-calling, it's only going to remind me of the good times. A sponsor once asked a sponsee a question: "What's the most important word in this phrase from the Big Book? 'Remember that we deal with food – cunning, baffling, powerful!'" The sponsee replied, "Powerful?" "No." "Cunning?" "No." "Then it must be 'baffling'," the sponsee said. "No," said the sponsor. "The most important word is 'remember.'"

The most important message I can impart to you is that if this miraculous change can happen to me, it can happen to you. None of us who have long-term abstinence were born with a special abstinence gland that keeps us away from the food. No matter how many years we have done it, we all still do it the same way – one day at a time.

I was given a gift one day 20 years ago: a day, and then a week of abstinence after months and years of trying. This gift was not of my own doing, but a gift from my Higher Power. I also understand that _he_ won't take it away from me, _I_ will have to actively throw it away. I don't want to do that. I don't want to overeat today, and I also don't want to _want_ to overeat today. The key to being free of the urge to eat is working the Steps.

That desire to remain free comes from long-term abstinence. I understand today something I couldn't see when I was slipping and sliding – getting and losing my abstinence every few months. What I understand is that long-term abstinence is light years ahead of that earlier way. It gives me a different perspective than I had during my previous, short term incidences of abstinence.

The real gift I got in my first week of abstinence was to stay away from the screaming desire to eat – which I know now was the voice of my disease, not me. The loud voice in my head was saying "you've only got a few days, you can start again tomorrow." When I look around at a room full of abstinent old-timers in program now, I realize one important thing: _none of them started their abstinence on a tomorrow._ I think if you asked them, almost all of them would tell you that sometime in their first week, the voices in their heads were also screaming for them to eat and to start over again tomorrow. Through the grace of their Higher Power, they were able to say "For today, I won't eat."

If you are still in the food, you've got to answer a simple question: *If not now, when?* Your disease will always throw the "tomorrow" mantra up in your face. If at some point you do get abstinent, you'll have to endure that voice of the disease screaming in your head to go eat. If you do it over and over before you get abstinent, you will have doubled, tripled or in some way multiplied that pain. Why not start today? It's as good as any other day.

Besides... *tomorrow never comes.*

A profound movie line came from that classic philosophical film, "The Muppet Movie": "*Life is a movie, write your own ending.*"

In closing, let me steal from the best:

"*Our book is meant to be suggestive only. We realize we know only a little. God will constantly disclose more to you and to us. Ask Him in your morning meditation what you can do each day for the man who is still sick. The answers will come, if your own house is in order. But obviously you cannot transmit something you haven't got. See to it that your relationship with Him is right, and great events will come to pass for you and countless others. This is the Great Fact for us.*

Abandon yourself to God as you understand God. Admit your faults to Him and to your fellows. Clear away the wreckage of your past. Give freely of what you find and join us. We shall be with you in the Fellowship of the Spirit, and you will surely meet some of us as you trudge the Road of Happy Destiny.

May God bless you and keep you - until then."

APPENDIX I – Helpful slogans and phrases

As a writer, I always tried to follow a writing teacher's advice: avoid clichés like the plague (although I'm sure you'll find this book riddled with them). However, many program slogans have great truth and while I have sprinkled them throughout this book, they are worth repeating. Here are a few:

We can't think our way into right acting, but we can act our way into right thinking.

Hurt people hurt people.

Don't just do something, stand there!

You can eat what you want, or you can get what you want.

I judge myself based on my intentions, while others judge me by my actions.

What other people think of me is none of my business.

Change isn't painful, resistance to change is painful.

If I focus on the problem, the problem increases. If I focus on the answer, the answer increases.

While Faith without Works is dead, Plans without Action is Fantasy.

If you are right, you have no need to be angry; if you are wrong, you have no right to be angry.

Never talk to yourself any worse than you'd talk to a child you love and care about.

Two of my favorites from an old-timer in Orange County, CA:

"The shortest distance to insanity is through comparison."

"I may not be much, but I'm all I think about."

APPENDIX II – Other helpful items

I'd like to recommend some extra reading for you, some of it program reading, and other things not program inspired.

Since the first edition of this book was published in 2014, I have written a number of essays on recovery from food addiction. The articles, as well as recordings of various talks and retreats can be found on my website: **www.foodrelapse.com**.

Another recommended piece of reading is the best 12 Step pamphlet ever written: *"A Member's Eye View to A.A.,"* which is available at A.A. meetings and online at the A.A. website.

Dr. Paul's story in the Big Book, *"On Acceptance."* It's a path for living. And don't just read "The Acceptance Paragraph," read the whole chapter – especially from "The Acceptance Paragraph" to the end of the chapter.

"Freedom from Bondage," also in the Big Book (page 544).

"A New Pair of Glasses," by Chuck C.

Al Anon: *A Checklist of our Maturity*

Al Anon: *The Do's and Don'ts*

Let me again mention the O.A. Los Angeles Intergroup's "Virtual Speakers Bureau." It was the first podcast in O.A. It is still going strong today with over 400 speaker files of all sorts. Many of the people on these podcasts have 20-plus years of abstinence. These are great to listen to if you live in an area where there are not strong meetings. They are also great to take with you when you are on the road or somewhere that makes going to any type of meeting impossible. In some places, meetings use these speakers as the main speaker at their meeting.

These podcasts can be found on the L.A. Intergroup website at: www.oalaig.org. They can also be accessed through various podcast clients, such as iTunes. In either case, there is no charge and they can be downloaded for later use.

Another very strong resource is a Big Book phone meeting group is the "A Vision for You" group. They have daily phone meetings, as well as Sunday "Special Edition" meetings. All of their meetings and Special Editions are also recorded and posted on their website for later listening. The "A Vision for You" website is: http://www.avision4you.info.

27666083R00117

Made in the USA
Columbia, SC
27 September 2018